Daughter of the Shtetl
The Memoirs of Doba-Mera Medvedeva

Jews of Russia & Eastern Europe and Their Legacy

Series Editor
MAXIM D. SHRAYER (Boston College)

Editorial Board
KAREL BERKHOFF
(NIOD Institute for War, Holocaust and Genocide Studies)
JEREMY HICKS
(Queen Mary University of London)
BRIAN HOROWITZ
(Tulane University)
LUBA JURGENSON
(Université de Paris IV—Sorbonne)
ROMAN KATSMAN
(Bar-Ilan University)
DOV-BER KERLER
(Indiana University)
VLADIMIR KHAZAN
(Hebrew University of Jerusalem)
ALICE NAKHIMOVSKY
(Colgate University)
ANTONY POLONSKY
(Brandeis University)
JONATHAN D. SARNA
(Brandeis University)
DAVID SHNEER
(University of Colorado at Boulder)
ANNA SHTERNSHIS
(University of Toronto)
LEONA TOKER
(Hebrew University of Jerusalem)
MARK TOLTS
(Hebrew University of Jerusalem)

Daughter of the Shtetl
The Memoirs
of Doba-Mera
Medvedeva

•

Translated by
ALICE NAKHIMOVSKY
Edited and introduced by
MICHAEL BEIZER
and ALICE NAKHIMOVSKY

BOSTON
2019

Library of Congress Cataloging-in-Publication Data

Names: Medvedeva, Doba-Mera, 1892-1976, author. | Nakhimovsky, Alice S., editor, translator, writer of supplementary textual content. | Beizer, M. (Mikhail), editor, writer of supplementary textual content.

Title: Daughter of the shtetl : the memoirs of Doba-Mera Medvedeva / translated by Alice Nakhimovsky ; edited and introduced by Michael Beizer and Alice Nakhimovsky.

Identifiers: LCCN 2018056648 (print) | LCCN 2018057747 (ebook) | ISBN 9781618115935 (ebook) | ISBN 9781618114358 (hardcover : alk. paper) | ISBN 9781618114365 (pbk. : alk. paper)

Subjects: LCSH: Medvedeva, Doba-Mera, 1892-1976. | Jews—Belarus—Khotsimski raion—Biography. | Jews—Russia (Federation)—Saint Petersburg—Biography. | Khotsimski raion (Belarus)—Biography. | Saint Petersburg (Russia)—Biography. | Jewish communists—Russia (Federation)—Saint Petersburg--Biography.

Classification: LCC DS134.93.M43 (ebook) | LCC DS134.93.M43 A3 2019 (print) | DDC 947.084092 [B]—dc23

LC record available at https://lccn.loc.gov/2018056648

Copyright © 2019 Academic Studies Press
All rights reserved.

ISBN 978-1-61811-435-8 (hardback)
ISBN 978-1-61811-436-5 (paperback)
ISBN 978-1-61811-593-5 (electronic)

Book design by Lapiz Digital Services
Cover design by Ivan Grave

Published by Academic Studies Press.
28 Montfern Avenue
Brighton, MA 02135, USA
press@academicstudiespress.com
www.academicstudiespress.com

The publication of this book was made possible by grants from the Hebrew University, Colgate University, and from Boston College.

Table of Contents

Acknowledgments	vii
Translator's Note	viii
My Babushka and Her Memoirs *Michael Beizer*	1
A Unique Memoirist in Turbulent Times *Alice Nakhimovsky*	9
A Diary of My Days *Doba-Mera Izrailevna Medvedeva (Gurevich)*	29
Index	147

Acknowledgments

Both of us give warm thanks to Michael Beizer's older sister Tema Slobodinskaia (Jerusalem), his cousin Veniamin Medvedev (St. Petersburg), the son of Aunt Ida, and his second cousin Anna Dymentman (Afula, Israel) for clarifying parts of family history and providing photographs. Michael Moz (Maale Adumim, Israel) was indispensable in providing Michael with copies of pages from the rabbinical books kept in the State Archives of the Briansk and Chernigov Regions.

Michael Beizer's late colleague and friend Natalia Vasilievna Yukhneva (Kunstkamera, St. Petersburg) was the first outside scholar to evaluate and publish Doba-Mera's memoirs in Russian in St. Petersburg. We are grateful for her abiding interest in the project. Thanks also go to her children, Yekaterina Yukhneva and Andrei Yukhnev, and to the Peter the Great Museum of Anthropology and Ethnography (Kunstkamera, St. Petersburg) for being so responsive in providing permissions.

ChaeRan Freeze of Brandeis was instrumental in getting the project off the ground and characteristically generous ever after. Thanks of many different kinds go to Maxim D. Shrayer (Boston College), Lyudmila Sholokhova (YIVO Institute), Arkadi Zeltser (Yad Vashem), Roberta Newman (YIVO Institute), Natasha Azava, Esq., Alexander Nakhimovsky (Colgate University), Keren Kishrei Mada at the Hebrew University, and the Colgate University Research Council.

Translator's Note

Because the notebooks are in Russian, and Doba-Mera herself wrote Yiddish names in the Russian manner, that is how they appear in English: for example, Girsh, not Hirsch, and Meilakh, not Meylakh. Sometimes she Russified names, and sometimes not; sometimes one half of a double name will be Russian and the other half more or less Yiddish—for example, Izrail´-Vel´ka. Doba-Mera was a real-life speaker negotiating language borders without being aware that she was engaged in a linguistic enterprise. We follow her choices. Transliterations are Library of Congress, with the exception of familiar names like Kerensky, which are spelled as they would be in a newspaper.

My Babushka and Her Memoirs

Michael Beizer

My maternal grandmother, Doba-Mera (Miriam) Medvedeva, née Gurevich, was born on the twenty-fifth of Heshvan, 5655 according to the Jewish calendar—November 15, 1892—in the shtetl of Khotimsk, in Klimovichi District of Mogilev Province (*guberniia*).[1] Doba-Mera was the daughter of an Enlightenment-influenced *melamed* named Izrail'-Vel'ka (Vol'f; 1865–1909) and his wife, Rokhl'-Leah Ben'iaminovna (née Medvedeva; 1868–1903). A melamed was a children's teacher in the traditional system of religious education, but in the only remaining photograph we see Izrail'-Vel'ka in European clothing and without a head covering.

Seventy percent of the shtetl's three thousand inhabitants were Jews. Evgenii Shifrin, from Klimovichi, put it this way: "A hundred years ago the trains bypassed Khotimsk, and they still do, as though Khotimsk were the edge of the earth, which may in fact be the case."[2] According to Liubov' Khazanova, who lived in Khotimsk in the 1920s: "It was a small town with single-story wooden houses. Very occasionally you'd see a brick one, but two-story houses were altogether only a handful. In the center was the market square, which had a big church; the synagogue was on a side street. The nearest railway station was in Kosiukovich, a city thirty-five kilometers away."[3]

---

1   Here and elsewhere, dates before 1918, when Russia switched to the Gregorian calendar, are given in Old Style—that is, according to the Julian calendar.
2   Quoted in Aleksandr Litin, "Mestechki Mogilevshchiny—ot evreiskoi unikal'nosti k polnomu zabveniiu" [The shtetelach of the Mogilev region, from Jewish uniqueness to total oblivion], in *Istoriia mogilevskogo evreistva: Dokumenty i liudi* [A history of the Mogilev Jews: Documents and people] (Minsk: Iunipak, 2006), 2:263.
3   Liubov' Solomonovna Khazanova, "Vospominaniia o rode Khazanovykh" [Recollections of the Khazanov family], manuscript; collection of the author.

Grandmother's father came from an ancient rabbinical line, the Syrkins, which includes the well-known Talmudist Yoel Sirkis (the Bach, 1561–1640) of Lublin, the author of *Bayit Chadash* (New House). As the family's second son, Izrail´-Vel´ka was fictively ascribed to a different family, the Gureviches. The Gurevich family had no other sons, which guaranteed that when Izrail´-Vel´ka reached draft age, he would get the exemption for only sons.

My grandmother's maternal great-grandfather, Khayim Yankel Medvedev, was registered in the 1811 census (revision list) as a twenty-nine-year-old town dweller of the city of Surazh, Chernigov Province.[4] His son Ben'iamin, born in 1821, was the father of my grandmother's mother. Ben'iamin had a wife named Rivka and eight children, the seventh of whom was Rokhl´-Leah. He lived in the village of Vlazovichi in Surazh District and was a man of some wealth. He had his own house and land and leased the estates of the merchant Golovin and the country squire (*pomeshchik*) Iskritskii, in whose house he settled his eldest son, Berka, and family. He kept an inn and engaged in farming. There were no Talmud scholars in their line.[5] Doba-Mera was only eleven years old when she lost her mother and sixteen when she lost her father. There had been no money to send her to the *gymnasium* (Russian preparatory school with a classical curriculum). The only school she ever attended was her father's *heder* (religious primary school), where she studied alongside boys. This was unusual but not impossible at that time in Lithuania and Belorussia.[6] As a little girl, she was profoundly distressed by her position as an outcast and her inability to get an education. In addition, from childhood on she performed burdensome household tasks for a variety of families. Everywhere she encountered extreme need, illness, greed, and wretchedness; very rarely, human kindness and sympathy. She lived through the revolution of 1905 and two pogroms and participated in illegal revolutionary activities. "I had no childhood, only years during which I was a child," she wrote many years later.

Because her father remarried and her stepmother had no love for the children from his first marriage, Doba-Mera was sent from one family of strangers to another. The year before her father's death she was taken on as part-relative,

---

4 State Archive of Briansk Province (GABO), *fond* (collection) 549, *opis´* (inventory) 2, *delo* (folder) 3, *listy* (pages) 153–54. Hereafter abbreviated, according to Russian convention, as f., op., d., and l. (singular) or ll. (plural).
5 State Archive of Chernigov Province, f. 127, op. 14, d. 4324, ll. 49–50.
6 Avraham Greenbaum, "The Girls' Heder and Girls in the Boys' Heder in Eastern Europe before World War I," *East/West Education* 18, no. 1 (1997): 55–62.

part-servant by her father's stepsister Gesia Belkina, who lived in Klintsy.[7] All this time, she was also responsible for her younger brother, Avrom-Yudl (Abram; 1894–1963). Her other brother, David (1902–1907), died in childhood. In 1910, at the age of seventeen, she married her second cousin—my grandfather, Meilakh Medvedev—who had been born on October 1 (29 Heshvan), 1890.[8] Meilakh's father, a *meshchanin* from Surazh by the name of Yankel-Moyshe (Iakov-Meisha) Berkovich (son of Berka [Borukh], 1868?–1914) Medvedev, opposed his son's marriage to a girl without a dowry.[9] Although he would not permit an engagement, he consented to have the orphaned girl live with the family, hoping this would quickly extinguish his son's love. If the marriage had not taken place, the young girl's reputation might have been ruined.[10] Formally it all ended well: the young couple married, had six children, and lived together for sixty-two years. But the trauma was not forgotten, and it is reflected in the memoirs, even though in Doba-Mera's circle things of this sort were supposed to remain unmentioned.

In the 1920s Grandfather kept a bakery in Klintsy and was therefore classified as a *lishenets* with limited civil rights.[11] After the end of the New Economic Policy (NEP), he, Grandmother, and their six children moved

---

7 The settlement of Klintsy was founded in 1707 by runaway sectarian (Old Believer) peasants. At the beginning of the twentieth century, it was part of Surazh District, Chernigov Province. According to the 1897 census, it had a population of 12,166, of whom 2,605 were Jews. At the beginning of the twentieth century, it supported seven large factories, one industrial plant, and up to a hundred small businesses. The town had three hospitals, five churches, three synagogues, sixteen elementary and high schools, including two gymnasiums and a technical school. It had a railway station, a diesel-powered electricity plant, a post office building with telephone and telegraph, two cinemas, two printing presses, a public library, and a newspaper, *Klintsovskaia gazeta* (http://klincy.narod.ru/chronicler.htm).
8 GABO, f. 585, op. 1, d. 1, l. 144.
9 A *meshchanin* in imperial Russia was a city dweller belonging to a taxable estate consisting of property owners, artisans, and merchants.
10 On Jewish marriage customs and the problems faced by Jewish brides in Russia, see ChaeRan Y. Freeze, *Jewish Marriage and Divorce in Imperial Russia* (Hanover, NH: University Press of New England, 2002), esp. chap. 1, "Creating the Jewish Family," 11–72.
11 The category *lishenets* (pl. *lishentsy*—a person deprived of something) first appeared in article 65 of the 1918 Soviet Constitution, in which "exploiters, people of the Church," and other representatives of the "old order" were deprived of the right to vote. With time, the category came to include artisans who employed even a single person, and together with the right to vote, *lishentsy* lost other fundamental rights, including those of free medical care, education, municipal housing, and registration in the labor market. Because of the specific pattern of Jewish employment (in trade and crafts), the percentage of *lishentsy* among them was particularly high.

from Klintsy to Leningrad.¹² It happened in the early 1930s. Only there, after the required period spent working in a factory and after enrollment in *rabfak* (workers' education courses), could the children of a *lishenets* count on obtaining a higher education. The grandparents themselves had no such opportunity to get an education. Grandfather worked as a transportation coordinator for the Lenin's Spark Leningrad Battery Works; Grandmother kept house and raised the children. My mother Rokhlya-Lea (Rakhil´) was born in the revolutionary year 1917.¹³ She was the third child. No sooner had she graduated from a high school for pharmacy than the Soviet-Finnish War broke out and she was sent to the front.¹⁴ She and my father registered their marriage in the "liberated" city of Vyborg.

In 1939, at the age of forty-seven, Grandmother decided that she had seen enough of life to begin a memoir. When she finished, she destroyed her account of the interwar Soviet period, which is a great pity but hardly surprising, if one considers the terrifying nature of those years for all of Leningrad.¹⁵ In addition, why remind the children that Papa had been a *lishenets* and had been "purged" from the Party? Better to end with a story of how he baked bread for the army of General Shchors.¹⁶

---

12 The New Economic Policy was a partial retreat from War Communism in favor of a market economy.
13 Rakhil´ (Rokhlya-Lea) Beizer (Medvedeva) (August 3, 1917, Klintsy–December 15, 2004, Jerusalem), GABO, f. 585, op. 1, d. 3, l. 346.
14 According to the August 1939 agreement between Germany and the USSR (the Molotov-Ribbentrop Pact), Finland was part of the Soviet sphere of influence. The Soviet government made territorial demands on the Finnish government and, when these were rejected, began military action in November 1939. In March 1940, after disproportionately heavy losses, the Red Army occupied Karelia and Vyborg, Finland's second largest city, which convinced Finland to sign a peace treaty.
15 The murder of Sergei M. Kirov, the first secretary of the Leningrad regional party organization on December 1, 1934, was followed by mass arrests, executions, and forced exiles, as a result of which the city's population diminished by thirty to forty thousand people. Even more mass repressions followed in 1937 and 1938.
16 In the Soviet historical literature, Nikolai Aleksandrovich Shchors (1895–1919) was a legendary commander of the Red Army and a hero of the Civil War. The Bohunsky Regiment of the First Ukrainian Soviet Division was formed under his command in September 1818 in the Unecha region, thirty-two kilometers from Klintsy. It was then that Shchors married Fruma Efimovna Rostova-Shchors (née Khaikina), from Unecha. On August 30, 1919, in the course of a battle against Denikin's White Army, Shchors was killed by a shot from behind at close range, probably delivered by Pavel Tankhil´-Tankhilevich, a representative of the Twelfth Army Revolutionary Military Council, acting on Leon Trotsky's orders.

It is worth pointing out that few people in the Soviet era had the courage to keep a diary or write memoirs, and those who did, as a rule, destroyed them. Such was the case with Grandmother's Khotimsk contemporary Mendel Khazanov (1890–1954). In the postwar years he started to write his memoirs, but he destroyed them in 1951 in the midst of a state-sponsored anti-Semitic campaign. "That's what all honorable people did then," explained his son, "because if the writer was arrested, then everybody mentioned in the memoir would end up in the cross-hairs of the security police."[17]

During World War II, in evacuation first in Orsk and later in Cheremkhovo, a coal mining town to the west of Lake Baikal, Grandmother gradually returned to religion. According to family legend, she vowed that she would observe the mitzvot (commandments) if her sons and sons-in-law returned safely from the front. And they did, although they were wounded (my father lost his arm). In the years of the Thaw, she again took up her memoirs, describing her impressions of the Finnish War and the first years of evacuation. Then, in 1958, she began a diary in which she described her golden wedding anniversary and her complicated relations with her children and husband.

I remember Grandmother and Grandfather's wooden house in Levashovo, a settlement outside Leningrad, where they moved after Grandpa retired in 1952, and where we often spent the summer. None of us grandchildren knew that the impenetrable green fence in the woods, which we were forbidden even to peek through, surrounded a former execution and burial site for twenty-eight thousand "enemies of the people."[18]

The house had no modern conveniences such as running water or a sewerage system. To get water, you had to take a bucket to the well. The grandchildren were kept away from the street for fear of rowdy anti-Semitic teenagers. As I now understand, both in the way it looked (dilapidated and neglected, with its tilted-over fence, its vegetable garden, its chickens, and, until Khrushchev forbade it, its resident female goat) and the kind of life that reigned there (Yiddish, kosher, the eternal quarrels and mutual support within a single large family that included at times not only cousins but second cousins)—that house in many ways was a remnant of the shtetl, accidentally transported to the outskirts of Leningrad and preserved right up until the 1970s.

---

17   Aleksandr Mendelevich Khazanov, "Memory," written in the United States, 2009; collection of the author.
18   Michael Beizer, *Evrei Leningrada 1917–1939: Natsional´naia zhizn´ i sovetizatsiia* [The Jews of Leningrad, 1917–1939: National life and Sovietization] (Moscow: Mosty kul´tury, 1999), 124–25.

This is how my older sister Tema remembers what happened with the goat: "Grandma hid one goat, but it bleated, and the neighbors informed on her. So up drove a black truck, and two men got out and asked Grandma, 'Where is your large horned piece of livestock?' Grandma stood in their path: 'Shoot me! I'm not handing over the goat.' But they didn't obey her. So we lost our goat milk, and it was five liters."[19] Grandmother was the main repository of tradition in our family. In addition to regular dishes, she kept separate kosher dishes for herself. On Friday nights candles were lit. Grandfather, a member of the Communist Party, prayed in a fraying *tales*, with *tfilin* (a new *tales* was impossible to get). He attended an illegal minyan (prayer group) in nearby Pargolovo, and sometimes went to the single working synagogue in Leningrad, which had 170,000 Jews—the Choral Synagogue on Lermontovskii Prospekt. On the doorpost of their bedroom was a mezuzah, which my cousin, Grandmother's beloved Venia—the only one of the younger grandsons who was circumcised—had to kiss before his violin examinations. What else could a Jewish child be expected to study? For Pesach Grandmother managed to collect together all or at least most of the family, including the Russian wife and Russian husband of two of her children, as well as thirteen grandchildren. So that we would all fit around the holiday table in the small dining room, they had to hold two seders. Of course, the dishes were special, Passover ones, and the wine was homemade, from raisins that were kosher for Passover. Grandmother gave us *tsimes* and *imberlakh* and made us listen to the Haggadah from beginning to end, together with her Russian commentary. In the early 1960s, when it was not possible to bake matzo in the synagogue, Grandmother baked it herself on the big kitchen stove that was heated with wood.

From time to time, Grandmother would try to teach us grandchildren the Hebrew alphabet and acquaint us with the important stories of the *Chumash* (the five books of Moses). Her "obscurantism" was vigorously resisted by the atheist children. Nonetheless, it was from her that I heard for the first time about the prophet Moses and the marvelous Joseph. When Grandmother and Grandfather died, she on the twenty-fourth of Adar, 5736 (February 25, 1976), and he in 1980, a whole trunk of *sifrei kodesh* (holy books) remained on their upper-floor balcony. The books had been brought to them by the children of old people who had died in Levashovo and Pargolovo.

---

19 The notes of Tema Slobodinskaia, 2007; personal archive of Michael Beizer.

My grandmother's memoirs survived the evacuation and were discovered by Aunt Ida, Venia's mother, who inherited the house in Levashovo.[20] In the summer of 2001, a few months before her death, during my visit to St. Petersburg, Ida gave me Grandmother's notebooks. She apparently felt that, as an Israeli historian, I was the most appropriate repository of family history.

In addition to being an important family document, the memoirs, in my opinion, also have historical value. As far as I know, these memoirs of a Lithuanian-Belorussian Jewish shtetl at the turn of the twentieth century—written by a poor, uneducated woman—are very unusual. Just as unusual is the power of her writing. Seen through the eyes of this unfortunate girl, shtetl life loses the romantic aura ascribed to it by people who had good lives there, as well as by postwar scholars carried away by nostalgia.[21] It is striking how a simple woman with no conception of feminism understood herself as a strong personality with things to say, whose experience could prove useful to her descendants. Her native intelligence and awareness are impressive.

Two ways of viewing life come together in Doba-Mera's memoirs: on the one hand, her tendency to present herself as a victim of circumstances—characteristic of women, orphans, representatives of discriminated-against minorities, and immigrants—and on the other, her emphatic determination to realize her right to a normal life. One can see in the memoirs a tendency to take revenge—although after the fact and in written form—against those who have offended her. The reader gets the impression that Doba-Mera's frequent changes in her place of work and her participation in revolutionary activity were attempts to escape loneliness and acquire a circle of friends who might take the place of a family. Unfortunately, she was unable to do this before her marriage, and the marriage itself was not a very good one, at least in her estimation.

The text of the memoirs had to be edited to make it easily readable. Russian was not, after all, Doba-Mera's native language, but she avoided writing in Yiddish, seeing that it was going out of use. Certainly the narrative devices at Grandmother's disposal were limited; she depended on ideas and patterns of expression common in her society and in the mass media. It is no accident that in his book *How Our Lives Become Stories*, Paul John Eakin

---

20 Ida (Eidlia) Meilakhovna Medvedeva (December 1, 1924, Klintsy–September 5, 2002, St. Petersburg).
21 In this sense, the present text is the complete opposite of the memoirs of Pauline Wengeroff (*Memoirs of a Grandmother: Scenes from the Cultural History of the Jews of Russia in the Nineteenth Century*, vol. 1 (Stanford, CA: Stanford University Press, 2010)

asks, "How much of what autobiographers say they experience is equivalent to what they really experience, and how much of it is merely what they know how to say?"[22] Nevertheless, autobiography is not fiction; it is not completely made up, as some deconstructionists imagine. In the case of a naive writer like Doba-Mera Medvedeva, the notion of autobiography as fiction is even less relevant. Presented from the point of view of an outcast, put through the prism of traditional shtetl culture with its sprinkling of "class consciousness" and atheism, filtered through self-censorship and ideas of morality, her memoirs are nonetheless—discounting only her repetition of rumors that she could not verify—based on the real facts of her own life. They may help us to rethink our ideas about the Jewish shtetl in the Pale of Settlement.

---

22 Paul John Eakin, *How Our Lives Become Stories: Making Selves* (Ithaca, NY: Cornell University Press, 1999), 4.

A Unique Memoirist in Turbulent Times

Alice Nakhimovsky

Doba-Mera Medvedeva belongs to a vanishingly small group of memoirists who are neither elite nor highly literate but whose observations from the ground cast a vivid light on a lost world. A born storyteller whose first language was Yiddish, Doba-Mera kept Russian-language notebooks to preserve her past for her Russian-speaking grandchildren. Her focus is the shtetl, the rural town in which Jews, legally confined to the Russian Pale of Settlement, lived their lives. For some Jews, particularly Americans distant in time and place from Doba-Mera, the shtetl is an object of nostalgia, a place where Jews lived like Jews and among Jews (notwithstanding a little anti-Semitic violence). Doba-Mera shows us the quarrelsome underside of that life. She does this not because she was a revisionist—there was nothing for her to revise—but because divisiveness was the driving force of her experience. Through her, we see family antagonisms in a time of scarce resources. We see her attempts to break free through work, revolution, and, eventually, marriage. Doba-Mera's life encompassed two pogroms and two world wars. Yet she endured, remembered, and wrote.

Because of Doba-Mera's economic fragility, a condition that underlies her many resentments, she saw what people from more privileged classes could not and often did not see. Because she was a woman, when she writes about education, apprenticeship, courtship, or the dynamics of Marxist circles in 1905, what she is giving us is a woman's view. There are very few memoirs from someone of her background: people like Doba-Mera were not used to setting down their thoughts in writing and were not conditioned to think that their memories of everyday life would be of interest to anyone else. It is not accidental that the only comparable memoirs we have, collected in groundbreaking anthologies by Jeffrey Shandler (*Awakening Lives: Autobiographies of Jewish Youth in*

Poland before the Holocaust) and Jocelyn Cohen and Daniel Soyer (*My Future Is in America: Autobiographies of Eastern European Jewish Immigrants*)—came about because the leadership of YIVO, the Institute for Jewish Research, set up a writing contest whose actual purpose was to get people who otherwise would not have done so to write about their lives.[1] These memoirs provide significant context for Doba-Mera's, but there are also poignant differences. The YIVO memoirs that originated in America are all almost celebratory. Early difficulties—even the difficulties of a boy who was, like Doba-Mera, an orphan—are overcome. The future is bright. The Polish memoirs also look forward to the future although, as far as we know, not a single one of those young writers survived the war. Doba-Mera is the only one of these naïve memoirists whose life extends into the Soviet period. When she thinks back, she is angry. This may be just her reaction, but one must not discount the Soviet conditions under which she lived. Even her memoirs weren't safe from those in power: the first 257 pages of her second notebook, about the period from the Soviet takeover until 1937, were torn out and presumably burned.

For the reader seeking an accurate idea of everyday life, Doba-Mera's kind of naïve writing has both values and pitfalls. What she observes is intentionally subjective, and often passionately so. Her relatives probably had a different take on some events. But a million everyday details do not play a role in her argument: they are there because they are background, and she is a writer who likes to describe. How did the loan economy work in a shtetl? What was the procedure for a sick person who could not pay to get care at a hospital? What were the interactions between a man's tailor (Doba-Mera), working at her sewing machine two steps from someone's kitchen, and her employer's wife? Where did apprentices eat, how did they get tipped, and what did they do with the money? How did courtship unfold as parents lost authority?

Not everything that Doba-Mera says is accurate, and not everything she reports is firsthand. As Michael Beizer points out, she writes authoritatively about who started a pogrom even through she was in hiding as it was going on. The reader is urged to check the notes, which sort through some

---

1   Jeffrey Shandler, *Awakening Lives: Autobiographies of Jewish Youth in Poland before the Holocaust* (New Haven: Yale University Press, 2002); Jocelyn Cohen and Daniel Soyer, *My Future Is in America: Autobiographies of Eastern European Jewish Immigrants* (New York: New York University Press, 2006). According to ChaeRan Freeze and Jay Harris, *Everyday Jewish Life in Imperial Russia: Selected Documents, 1772–1914* (Waltham, MA: Brandeis University Press, 2013), women like Doba-Mera speak through court documents and petitions but not as memoirists.

of these discrepancies. At the same time, it would be wrong to dismiss her accounts as nothing more than rumor. Fact-checking journalism did not exist in the small towns of the Pale. Rumor was part of the fabric of life, particularly in a time and place where journalistic accounts were not widely available, and certainly not in small towns in the Pale. People took action, for better or worse, in response to what they heard.

Myths were also woven into the fabric of life. They form a part of Doba-Mera's worldview, and she uses them to shape her narrative. A striking example is an idealized picture of a peasant in one of the stories she tells. Still a girl, Doba-Mera has been sent to board with an uncle and is traveling with her orphaned brother in a peasant wagon. The uncle is not happy to see them and, as she understands it, does not espouse Jewish values even on the eve of an important Jewish holiday. But the peasant coachman espouses exactly those values and knows enough to call out the Jews. "Ven´iaminovich!" he says. "Fear God! Tomorrow is your big Jewish fast. The Day of Judgment. How are you going to fast before God if you chase away these little orphans, your sister's children?"

Can we take this clash of saintly peasant/tightfisted Jewish relative at face value? Perhaps not. But we can see here Doba-Mera's quite sophisticated use of literary juxtapositions and her absorption of the Russian idea of the downtrodden peasant as morally noble. It also worth noting that as a naïve writer untroubled by issues of consistency, Doba-Mera deploys a myth when she needs it and dispenses with it when she doesn't. Her description of interethnic relations during the pogrom in Khotimsk is much more nuanced. A stove maker who knows the family will help them, but only up to a point, and everybody knows what that point is:

> [Father] took my brothers and me by the hand and led us by way of the kitchen gardens to a Russian stove maker we knew. This was "our" stove maker; he often did work for us . . . [but] when the shops were looted and the Russians started hauling Jewish things through the streets, our stove maker also wanted a little action, and we were holding him back. He started to send us home, saying that nothing was left (the pogrom was over).

Family

From the opening pages of the memoir, family dominates. Because Doba-Mera has hardly any schooling, there is no institution that shapes her. Until she starts working (and the shops in which she works, set in their owner's houses, are themselves barely removed from family), her relatives define the context in which her life unfolds. They rely on each other but prey on each other also: there is nobody she needs more or hates more.

Illness and death are a constant, resulting in family units that constantly shift. Doba-Mera's mother dies when she is eleven, leaving her, in Jewish terms, an orphan responsible for her two younger brothers, one of them not yet weaned. Life with a resentful stepmother is difficult, and at one point it looks like they will lose their father as well: the stepmother goes back to her parents, the father joins them, and a butcher's family moves into the house to look after the children. It's not clear in the text who feeds them for half a year, only that the butcher was not obligated to. In time the father and stepmother return, but five years later he himself dies. At sixteen Doba-Mera becomes responsible for her surviving brother.

Another constant is intrafamily struggles over two resources: the family's small house (really a cabin: a kitchen and two rooms) and the father's coveted seat in the synagogue. Food is another resource: in the story about the peasant coachman cited earlier, the reason a well-meaning neighbor sends the children to their uncle for the Jewish holidays is so they can *eat*. Yet even as some people contest resources, others share: in this world family members (and sometimes Jews more broadly) constitute the only safety net available. In the excerpt below, Doba-Mera and her brothers, just rejected by their uncle, are welcomed by an aunt:

> And so we reached the house of Aunt Gesia Belkina. There was nobody home but a servant. She was a Jewish servant, young and dark-complexioned. The driver explained to her that we were the mistress's relatives and that we were frozen and hungry orphans, and she was happy to take us in. The driver was happy that we were finally off his hands. He left quickly. Zlata—that was the cook's name—fed us and warmed us up, as attentive as though we were her family.

Taken out of context, the two excerpts suggest a simple moral world: a mean uncle is balanced by a kind aunt; the mean uncle is confronted by a compassionate Russian coachman, while in the house of the kind aunt there is a loving Jewish servant. When Doba-Mera wrote down this particular story, she probably wanted to emphasize the stark contrasts. But elsewhere some of these people and their interactions are more complicated and realistic.

The aunt, Gesia, plays a largely but not unerringly good role in Doba-Mera's life. Her backstory had its own complications: Gesia came into wealth when her brother-in-law Alter married her off against her will to another brother-in-law, who had just been widowed. Alter's scheming didn't have Gesia's welfare in mind so much as his own: in Doba-Mera's analysis, by arranging Gesia's marriage, he got both her and her mother out of the house they shared and, because the brother-in-law was rich, connected himself to a reliable source of funds. Alter, in Doba-Mera's view, is hateful. On the one hand, Gesia often backs Alter, the man who stole the synagogue seat from Doba-Mera's father and tried to take their house as well. On the other hand, when Doba-Mera needs help, it is Gesia who supplies it.

What is true in the family—help offered but in a complicated way—extends to Russian-Jewish society at large. When Doba-Mera's father is diagnosed with cancer, she travels with him to Kiev, to the Brodskii Hospital, "maintained by rich Jews for poor ones." In employing this phrase, Doba-Mera isn't expressing gratitude so much as briefly suspending the class resentment that is a fundamental part of her worldview. It's nice that help is offered, but too bad that getting it is so difficult. That this hospital is in Kiev, where most Jews are not legally permitted to live, is an additional complication. Can it be overcome? Yes, like many legal barriers in imperial Russia, it gives way under the combined forces of Jewish unity and Russian susceptibility to bribes. The Russian state doesn't want Jews in Kiev, so the police stage raids on people without documents. Readers of Sholem Aleichem's Menachem Mendel stories will remember a raid like that, turned into comedy. Doba-Mera's accounts of undocumented Jews in Kiev are by contrast anguished, though in the excerpt below, thanks to bribery, a comic note creeps in:

> During the time that we lived in the apartment, there were a number of raids that our host found out about before they happened. He would send us out to the street. One day there was an unexpected shout: "Raid!" What should we do? I myself could dash out, but there wasn't time to get Father ready. . . . Father was lying there, terrified. He, poor man, was not worried about himself but about me. I calmed him down and asked what had happened. He said that the host had curtained him off with a sheet and told him to cover his head. When the policeman asked who was there, the host answered that it was a woman in labor. The policeman took a look, and since he couldn't see a man's face, he left. Apparently he and the host had an agreement not to bother sick people.

So bribes work. The other feature of Russian-Jewish life, a certain grudging mutual support, makes it likely that illegal Jews will find lodging with legal ones and even get loans from them. When Doba-Mera and her father leave for Kiev, Gesia gives them a letter "to a rich relative, asking for her help if it turned out that we could not find a way to support ourselves." The recipient of the letter is indeed a relative, albeit one so distant that she doesn't even know that Doba-Mera exists (and from the tone of the story, couldn't care less). Nevertheless, she advances the money with the expectation that Gesia will repay her. However unwillingly, the obligation of mutual support is honored.

Values

Doba-Mera's values fall into three groups: traditional Jewish, universal (she honors kindness, peacemaking, generosity), and Russian-secular. A touch of Marxism supports her genuine, although not wholly consistent, preference for the poor over the rich.

The traditionally Jewish strain is the easiest to see. Her family has *yiches*— an enviable lineage of learned men. Aware of her Russian-speaking children and grandchildren and even more of the Soviet conditions under which she wrote, Doba-Mera doesn't use the Yiddish term. But anyone familiar with the concept can see it looming behind the pride she takes in her background. In the world of Doba-Mera's childhood, yiches is better than wealth. When she writes of her father "his line of our family was highly respected but poor," she is using a commonplace trope, elevating the status of the poorest man in a way that the richest will have to appreciate. Doba-Mera's description of her background takes a dig at the merchant class as well, since their status on the Jewish ladder was also below that of scholar. If a family has no scholars, then it can still pride itself on not making a living from artisanal trades like tailoring. So she points that out too:

> Grandpa was a rabbi of the eighteenth generation. They were important people, very learned. There were no businessmen or craftsmen among them. My mother's family was better known, because in the first place the family was large, and second, everyone was in business, so almost all of them were rich.

Her father was a melamed, a teacher of small children. The profession was of low prestige: on the one hand, a melamed had to be learned, but on the other, he was irredeemably poor, teaching in his own home from morning to night, Jewish holidays excepted, and constantly struggling to extract tuition from parents who were no better off than he was.[2] Morally, her father shone. Doba-Mera makes a particular point of his empathy with the poor:

> When he was in the synagogue, he didn't want to sit in a place of honor—that is, by the *mizrah*, the eastern wall. He always found a place with the artisans and the paupers, who sat in the middle of the synagogue and by the doors and the reading stand in the center, since paupers and artisans were not allowed in the place of honor.

The other aspect of her father that Doba-Mera venerates is his connection to secular Yiddish and Russian culture. Although once again she doesn't use the word, her father is a *maskil*, a proponent of secular knowledge. After hours he teaches arithmetic to children who hope to pass the entrance exams for Russian schools. He follows politics, reads literature in both Yiddish and Hebrew, and participates in Yiddish theater. He organizes a credit union for his fellow teachers and a bank that provides loans to traveling salesmen, to protect them from the rich. There is no virtue that he lacks except his acquiescence to his children's treatment by their shrewish (in Doba-Mera's presentation) stepmother. She records this but forgives him.

Religion

Neither the beliefs nor the practices of Judaism play much of a role in the text. Perhaps because of the Soviet era in which Doba-Mera wrote, perhaps because of her own involvement in Marxism, which we will get to shortly, she writes without a hint of sentimentality about Sabbaths and holidays—an option that would not have implied belief in God. More surprisingly for a woman writer, she barely talks about preparing for them. The references that are in the text are negative. We know she has to clean on Thursday nights, which is burdensome. Lack of money makes buying food for the Sabbath a weekly problem. She has to buy it late, when the prices go down. Knowing this, from the house next door Alter's wife keeps a vigilant eye out to see if Doba-Mera's cooking starts so late that the Sabbath is violated:

---

2   This somewhat surprising fact is attested to in multiple sources. See Shaul Stampfer, *Families, Rabbis, and Education: Traditional Jewish Society in Nineteenth-Century Eastern Europe* (Oxford: Littman Library of Jewish Civilization, 2010), 32.

> Aunt Lyfsha next door would be looking to see if I lit the stove late on Friday, although that would be because before that I didn't have the money to buy [food for the Sabbath]. The sun would go down, and I would have to go hungry that day and the next. She didn't ask why I was lighting the stove late but threatened that she would pour water on it.[3]

There is no talk about special foods for Sabbath or holidays. Food plays a big role in this memoir and is often cited quite specifically but only in two contexts: it is either withheld (by the stepmother, primarily) or offered to someone out of love, in a time of illness or serious need. Otherwise, Jewish holidays are simply a way of marking time. This function disappears around 1905, when Doba-Mera is absorbed in Marxist circles (the May 1 holiday replaces it), but resurfaces after she marries. It is worth reiterating, from the introduction of Michael Beizer, Doba-Mera's grandson, that after World War II Doba-Mera returned to Judaism, becoming an anomaly for her children and in Soviet society as a whole. But this turn of events is not predictable from her notebooks.

Education

It is not surprising that the only Sabbath ritual Doba-Mera recalls with warmth is likely a violation of it. When she was ten or eleven, she reports,

> three of us—me, Fania Rubinchik, and Dasha Blanter—decided to teach poor Jewish girls to read and write. Why Jewish? Because there was a school for Russians, and Jews weren't accepted there. And so on Saturday, almost all the little girls from our shtetl would gather at the Rubinchiks', and we taught them to read and write and gave them homework.

Doba-Mera was able to do this teaching because from the age of six she had been a pupil in her father's heder (religious primary school) where she learned reading and writing. It was not unusual for girls to go to heder. If they wanted to continue beyond this elementary level, they were either tutored at home—generally in Jewishly irrelevant subjects like arithmetic, writing, and history—or went to a modern Yiddish-, Hebrew-, or Russian-based private

---

3   A neighbor catches a Sabbath violation from an open door in Chaim Grade, *My Mother's Sabbath Days* (New York: Knopf, 1986), 23, although in this case, the observer is the memoirist's saintly mother, and she refrains from saying anything.

school. But the school option was mostly available in large cities, and in any case, Doba-Mera's family could not have afforded it. Instead, she reports with some pride that her father tutored her himself, despite knowing how useless this would be for a girl:

> He taught me himself, as I said, and gave me an education in Yiddish, Russian, and Hebrew. He himself taught me the real Talmud, which was absolutely off-limits to girls, and the history of the Jews in Hebrew. This "higher learning," as he called it, was given only to boys, but since I was bright, and there was no other kind of education he could give me, he didn't, as he said, have the heart to tear me away from my studies. He understood perfectly well that an education in the Talmud wouldn't do anything for my future. But he nevertheless decided that this was better than no education at all, because he loved education and used to say about me: "Let her study; it won't hurt her in her future life; it won't weigh her down."

Doba-Mera's educational idyll is broken by the combined juggernauts of her difficult life: her mother's death, her stepmother's ill will, the family's poverty, and the Russian state.

While boarding with Aunt Gesia, she becomes friends with a girl named Liza who is about to start the fifth grade in a gymnasium, a Russian preparatory school. Doba-Mera begins studying for the entrance exams—unaware, she says, that people in her position "don't get past the gymnasium door." This crushing truth is revealed to her first by Liza and subsequently by an actual school doorman. Later a different Jewish girl explains

> that our tsar and his officials didn't like Jews and made life hard for them in every way. Educational institutions had Jewish quotas of only 5 to 10 percent. Only the rich got in. They could even get nothing but Cs on the entrance exams and then study poorly; no matter what, they wouldn't be expelled. And she herself got in because her mama sews for free for the head of the gymnasium.

Back with her stepmother, Doba-Mera is not allowed to take even free Russian lessons. Her father buys her a textbook, Dmitrii Ilovaiskii's *Russian History*; her stepmother discovers it "and screamed at Father: why was he wasting money on me?" But the general idea that education is wasted on a poor girl was also a tenet of Aunt Gesia's family. Gesia's mother, Doba-Mera's step-grandmother, has no sympathy for the thirteen-year-old: "You're not Minkin's daughter [Liza], and you're not a Belkin [Gesia, by marriage]. You are a poor orphan. and Auntie has decided to send you to apprentice with a seamstress so you can earn your own bread."

Work

Indeed, Doba-Mera is sent out as an apprentice to a women's seamstress. Apprentices were basically tuition-paying servants, and in this particular shop they learned very little. In the excerpt below, as elsewhere, Doba-Mera's description of working conditions—exploitation combined with arbitrariness—is detailed and sharp:

> [The seamstress, Sosha,] had almost a dozen girl pupils and two master apprentices, a junior one and a senior one. Nobody bothered to teach us anything. She herself was a widow and the sole support of two sons and a daughter. The older one was a coppersmith who worked for an artisan, the younger one was a clerk in a store, and the daughter studied at the gymnasium. We pupils were supposed to prepare the irons and do all the housework, including washing floors and running errands. But we weren't taught to sew. The senior apprentice was good to us, and without the boss's knowledge she would let us sew something and showed us how. But she soon left.

Back at Doba-Mera's father's house—in general, changes of venue in this text are constant and dizzying—the decision is made to apprentice Doba-Mera to a men's tailor, as the learning period is shorter and the tuition cheaper. As a girl among fellow workers who are mostly young men, she encounters some rough language but otherwise records mostly friendship and good will. In one instance, as winter approaches, her compatriots see that she has no coat because it was taken in a pogrom; they buy her one (she later pays them back). In another, the boss's wife tries to get her to scrub floors, an ever-present danger as the workshops are all in the owner's living quarters and a girl's usefulness in housework is assumed. This demeaning extra assignment doesn't happen because the other workers make a fuss, and they have leverage: they can leave.

The memoir tells us a lot about working conditions in outlying towns in the early years of the twentieth century. Although Doba-Mera tends to resent her employers as rich, they are themselves often barely past extreme impoverishment.[4] Sometimes employers offer room and board; sometimes workers live and eat elsewhere, as Doba-Mera does even when working in Khotimsk, where she lives (she finds this a cause of shame). Work is seasonal. Employers sometimes fail to pay, but as just noted, workers can simply quit. Doba-Mera quits and changes jobs repeatedly.[5]

A Young Artisan as Radical

Doba-Mera's first year of apprenticeship and work comes in the revolutionary year 1905. She is still thirteen. But street life beckons with strikes and speeches. As a worker—even an apprentice—she is for the first time in her life the object of somebody's interest and respect. It is exhilarating and above all, again for the first time, fun:

> September passed. The month of October began. Strikes broke out. Some people came to see us and said, "Comrades! The workers in all the factories of our city are on strike. We, as tailors, must also stop working as a sign of solidarity with them. . . ." We didn't understand what was going on. "But we're just learning," we said. "We're not getting paid; in fact, we're paying to learn. What should we do?" They told us that we were the same as workers, since with the help of those who were learning, a boss could get away without hiring workers. Hearing that answer, we solemnly set off for home. We liked the whole scene. The streets were full of people. Everyone was dressed in their best clothes. People were walking in crowds, talking loudly, arguing.

The demonstrations are dangerous. Cossacks, the Russian Empire's riot squads, beat up demonstrators and, according to rumor, tie people to the tails of their horses and gallop away, dragging their victims along the cobblestones.

---

4   In *The World of Our Fathers* (New York: Harcourt Brace Jovanovich, 1976), Irving Howe quotes the Yiddish poet and editor Abraham Liessen, who observes that in Western Europe "workers struggle against capitalists who are very wealthy, while in our Jewish towns and cities, workers struggle against paupers like themselves" (22).
5   An employer who fails to pay is sued in Freeze and Harris, *Everyday Jewish Life in Imperial Russia*, 471.

This is frightening, but Doba-Mera is drawn to it. She doesn't ask anyone's permission to go out.

As the strikes start, she learns a new word, *shtreykbrekher*: she has no idea what it means, but it sounds menacing. She likes the fact that radicals "used words that not everybody understood." From this beginning, the narrative of her radicalization is tied up with the education that she so badly wants. A young man named Liova appears in her shop. He is a tailor but looks like an intellectual. He gives her pamphlets to read in Yiddish and Russian, which explain her social and economic condition and show how it can be changed. Together she and Liova read a book by Marx. She joins a radical group, leads a reading circle, and goes to clandestine meetings in the woods. There she and a girlfriend do guard duty, looking out for police and "directing comrades to the meeting while we ourselves picked wildflowers without arousing the suspicion of anybody passing by."

Young Jews radicalized in around the same years as Doba-Mera generally chose between Jewish organizations with Jewish goals—diaspora-territorialist, labor, Zionist—and non-Jewish ones; organizations with the second profile either had no interest in Jews whatsoever or believed that Jewish suffering would disappear with the triumph of the revolution, along with everybody else's. Although Doba-Mera records a meeting at which these conflicting approaches are debated, she herself does not seem to differentiate. A Marxist radical with the last name Shifrin, who introduces her to Liova, reappears at another point in the narrative as a martyr who has died in an act of Jewish self-defense against pogromists. At his funeral mourners sing the Yiddish song "You Fell Victim," which she quotes in full. Other solutions to the "Jewish question"—Zionism and emigration—also appear in the text, though briefly. Emigration in particular is raised as a possibility but doesn't happen, either because she is afraid or, as she claims in the text, because she feels bound by a promise she made to her husband's parents as a condition for allowing their engagement.

Marriage and the Maelstrom of History

Despite two pogroms, the death of her father, and her unceasing work in one tailoring shop or another, Doba-Mera's radical period was the happiest of her early life. Still, whatever radicalism provided to her—education, independence, a sense of possibility—dissipated well before the Bolsheviks took power. World War I drove off thought of anything but survival. She barely marks its transformation into the Russian Civil War. When the Bolsheviks arrive, her primary concerns are the chaos of people racing to evacuate, and the particular threat to Jews:

> The Black Hundreds started a rumor in the city that the Bolsheviks would start killing Jews first, since they were always the victims of disorder. The Jewish poor reacted to this provocation by leaving...and [they] took off in unknown directions. This happened in December, and the winter was cold, so many people suffered harshly for their recklessness. I remember how we nervously stood at the gates and watched the endless wagons of people of different types making their escape.

She and her husband bake bread for the Red Army, and the commander Nikolai Aleksandrovich Shchors himself comes to take a look. At the conclusion of her narrative about the Civil War, which constitute the final pages of her first notebook, she praises the secret police for bringing order: "But the Cheka figured things out quickly and would say to the informant, 'if your accusations turn out to be false, then the punishment meant for the guilty party will be yours.' And people started to inform on each other less frequently." She expresses no hope that the new government will fulfill its promise, because by the time she wrote those words, in 1939, she knew it wouldn't.

The first 257 pages of Doba-Mera's second notebook are missing. That they refer to family anguish during the Terror years is clear by the sentence on page 258, which Doba-Mera underlined and then crossed out. Michael Beizer deciphered it:

> At this point I became convinced that our life had just entered a period of calm, but that the slightest disturbance would make it erupt like a volcano. That period of calm was because there were no causes or instigators, but if there were any, the troubles would come back at us with great severity.

Her earlier words about the Cheka could be no more than dutiful—political insurance in case the notebooks fell into the wrong hands. What she actually had to say about her family's experience of the late 1930s, we will never know.

From 1910, the year of her marriage, the bulk of Doba-Mera's story is once again about family. Privately there is illness and varieties of mutual antagonism; in the public sphere there is war. She presents herself as not particularly enamored of her husband-to-be, a distant relative. Other suitors in the narrative come off better. She pictures herself as being pushed into the marriage by her sense of solidarity with her future husband in the face of his parents' opposition (because she was without a dowry). She and her husband do not appear to have been happy together, although they had six children and remained a couple to the end of their lives.

When World War II broke out, Doba-Mera and her husband, Meilakh Medvedev, were living in Leningrad. She was evacuated to safety in Siberia; Meilakh chose to remain in Leningrad with his factory and survived the siege. But well before the siege was lifted—just six months into the war, at the end of 1941—Doba-Mera got word of the destruction of the Jews:

> From places under German occupation came terrible news. They said that all the Jews had been annihilated. More grief. Grandmother, my sisters, my sister Meita, and the other relatives, and in general everybody was a blood relation. My heart broke into pieces.

In the face of this kind of death, quarrels are irrelevant. Earlier she saw Jewish life in all its fractiousness. In death everybody is family.

Fig. 1 Izrail'-Vel'ka (Vol'f) Gurevich. Klintsy, circa 1900.

Fig. 2 Wedding of Doba-Mera and Meilakh. Klintsy, 1910.

Fig. 3 Meilakh sitting second from the right with his mother Khaia-Reize and his brothers and sisters. Klintsy, late 1920s.

A Unique Memoirist in Turbulent Times | 25

Fig. 4 Doba-Mera and Meilakh with children. Standing from left to right: Masha, Izrail' (Zaia)-Vel'ka, Rakhil'; sitting: Isaak (Isia), Ida. Leningrad, circa 1933.

Fig. 5 Doba-Mera and Meilakh. Gold Wedding. Leningrad, 1960.

Fig. 6 Meilakh and Doba-Mera with children Zaia and Masha. Klintsy, 1916.

Fig. 7 Rakhil' and Sasha (Srul') at Soviet-Finnish war. 1939.

Fig. 8 Doba-Mera and Meilakh with older grandchildren. Standing from left to right: Vladimir (Vova) Berezovskii, Tema Beizer, Eduard (Edik) Medvedev. Sitting: Zina Medvedeva, Roza Medvedeva, Vladimir (Vova) Medvedev, Roza Beizer. Leningrad, 1948.

Fig. 9 Ida Medvedeva. Leningrad, 1946.

Fig. 10 The Medvedevs' house in Levashovo. 1990s.

A Diary of My Days

Doba-Mera Izrail´evna Medvedeva (Gurevich)

September 25, 1939

I decided a long time ago to write a memoir for my children, a diary of my days, to record at least the most memorable moments of my life. I am not very old, but I have seen much grief, and almost every day my life has been filled with so many interesting events and thoughts and feelings that I often go over them in my mind. So if I live into old age and sometimes open this notebook that I wrote in the past, I will read it with interest. And so will my children, who love me very much. Even though they don't seem much interested in their parents' past, and they already know a little bit about it, still I can present it more vividly in writing, so they will have both my memoir and my photograph. It is very painful to me that I have nothing left from my mother that would remind me of her. I do have my father's photo, and I look at it very often. It is dear to me as a memory of my beloved father with whom I was very close, and as a memory of my life with him.

So many times I have started to write, but different things pulled me away. Mostly I never had time, because I had to care for my family and every minute was precious. But I will call this notebook a diary and dedicate it to my children, and I will talk to it as I would talk to my only trusted, chosen friend; that is, my pen will record all my thoughts and memories. I will begin with the day of my birth, from the stories of my parents, from a time when I didn't remember anything and didn't understand. Later I will write from my own impressions.

I was born in Belorussia in the shtetl of Khotimsk, in what was then Mogilev Province. My father was a melamed: that is, a teacher who taught little children the basics of Jewish learning. My mother kept house. Let me say a few words about their habits and personalities. My mother was very pretty and had a beautiful figure. She was kind and gentle; I never heard her raise her voice. My father was the head of the family, as was the custom in the olden days.

He was very educated for his time, both in Jewish subjects and in Russian; he could read Latin. He took a great interest in politics and subscribed to the newspapers that were available then, as far as I can remember—*Der Fraynd*, *Ha-Melits*, and others—which was unusual for a shtetl in the middle of nowhere.[1] His beautiful curly auburn hair and beard made him look more like a poet than a melamed. He knew a lot of mathematics, and young people who hoped to pass "extern" exams for the gymnasium [preparatory school—MB] would come for help in solving problems when they got stuck, and he would always help them.[2]

He didn't like rich people. When he was in the synagogue, he didn't want to sit in a place of honor—that is, by the *mizrah*, the eastern wall. He always found a place with the artisans and the paupers, who sat in the middle of the synagogue and by the doors and the reading stand in the center, since paupers and artisans were not allowed in the place of honor. It sometimes happened that a wealthy artisan would buy a seat by the mizrah, at which point his wealthy neighbors would run away from him. And then there would be an uproar in the synagogue, both from the rich men and from the artisans and paupers, who would shout "They don't like us! Our money is *treyf* [not kosher—MB], because we earn it by our labor." The commotion would continue until the leaders of the synagogue (respected people, the heads of the Jewish community) would intervene and decide either to give the artisan back his money and leave the seat to the synagogue or make the rich man who couldn't stand his new neighbor buy the seat from him and keep it for himself. At that point the obedient artisan would take the money and rain down all the curses he knew on

---

1   *Der Fraynd* (The Friend), edited by Shaul Ginsburg, was the first daily Yiddish newspaper in Russia. It began publication in St. Petersburg in 1903, initially with a Zionist orientation. *Ha-Melits* (The Advocate) was a Hebrew newspaper founded in Odessa in 1860. At the time described here, it was a daily based in St. Petersburg under the editorship of Leon Rabinovich. It closed in 1904. Both newspapers were written for an educated audience.

2   Beginning in 1887, the so-called *numerus clausus* (quota system) restricted Jewish enrollment in high schools and institutes of higher education to 10 percent of the total number of students within the Pale of Settlement, 5 percent outside it, and 3 percent in the capital cities of St. Petersburg and Moscow. Some educational institutions accepted no Jews at all. Those who weren't accepted could study high-school or university subjects on their own and then sit for exams as externs (nonmatriculated students), in that way obtaining a high-school or university diploma. In 1909 the quota system was expanded to include externs, which cut off the path of most Jewish youth to a higher education. Secret but rigorous quotas restricting the admission of Jewish students were maintained at major private North American universities and colleges (Harvard, Columbia, Princeton, Colgate, etc.) until well after World War II.

his neighbor and the whole community, saying, "I don't even want to sit next to people like that." Or "You don't want me? You have an aversion to artisans? I'm no thief; I'll take you to court." And the affair would end up in court, before the head of the local zemstvo.[3] Whichever side could buy the judge off, that side would win. But if the place was awarded to the artisan, then usually either the rich man would leave or he would make peace with his new neighbor.

I've gotten off my topic a little. But as I was saying, my father loved artisans and poor people, and they loved and respected him. He taught poor children for free. Although the shtetl had a group of poor children whose tuition was covered by the Society to Aid the Poor, some parents were ashamed to send their children there.[4] So my father would teach them even though he was overwhelmed with work and would get up early and go to bed late, and spend all his time with the children. From seven to nine in the morning he taught children who were not in his class, and in the evening from eight to ten he worked with children who were not in his class, whereas from nine in the morning until eight in the evening, he worked with his main class, consisting of eight to ten children, mostly boys. Girls weren't usually sent to school, first because it was a waste of money, and second because parents in those days thought that girls did not need schooling. Why take a girl away from housekeeping? Especially given that once she grew up, she could be either a nanny or a seamstress, and in either case reading was unnecessary. Still, no matter how busy my father was, he always found time to read the paper, figure out what was going on in politics, and have a conversation about the Jewish question. There were a lot of Jewish questions. Later I'll describe what I remember about persecution directed against the Jews. My father also read a lot of literature, by both Jewish and Russian writers.

---

3   The zemstvo was a form of rural self-government instituted in 1864 in thirty-four provinces as part of the reforms of Alexander II. Not all provinces had zemstvos: they were not present in Mogilev but were in neighboring Chernigov (*Entsiklopedicheskii slovar'* (Encyclopedic dictionary) [St. Petersburg: Brokhaus & Efron, 1898], 9A:843). Each zemstvo was headed by a member of the local gentry, who acted as judge for peasants. In provincial towns this function was filled by members of the district court, appointed by the state (D. I. Raskin, "Istoricheskie realii rossiiskoi gosudarstvennosti i russkogo grazhdanskogo obshchestva v XIX-om veke" (Historical realities of Russian statehood and Russian civil society in the nineteenth century), in *Iz istorii russkoi kul'tury* (From the history of Russian culture) [Moscow, 1966], 5:741).
4   By "there," Doba-Mera means the Talmud Torah, a community-supported religious primary school attended by orphans and poor boys, while children from more prosperous families went to heder. Izrail'-Vel'ka ran a heder in his home.

Household tasks he saved for holidays. He performed such tasks twice a year: before Passover and during the autumn Jewish holidays. That was when he worked on the house. He even did carpentry himself, which astonished everyone. I remember how he built a pair of walls that connected two separate houses. He cut the logs himself and layered them with moss. People would stop and look with astonishment and ask how he knew how to do all this. He had good health and an even better mind.

Also my father was a good community man and organizer. For example, he organized all the melameds in his shtetl into a mutual loan fund. Every melamed put ten to twenty-five rubles into the fund, depending on what he could afford, and when one of them was in need, then he got a loan, say, one hundred rubles for ten months. The interest was low, just enough to run the fund. This fund helped poor melameds in dire circumstances. For instance, somebody in the family or the melamed himself fell ill, or he needed to buy wood for the winter or repair his house; there were many such reasons. In those days, if you got a loan from someone of means, then you had to hand over something valuable and pay a lot of interest, and there were instances when people kept the valuables on various pretexts. So this was a small fund, which they called *hevre gmiles hesed*, which means "loan association."

He also set up a savings and loan association. This was a real bank, which lent money to all the shtetl's poor. Even though many shtetls had such banks, our rich men were in no hurry to set one up and didn't even want one, because it would operate to their disadvantage for one simple reason. All the Jews of our shtetl, with the exception of some artisans, traveled around the local villages collecting raw materials and scrap iron. Since you needed money for this, and they were for the most part poor, the rich people gave them money. In exchange the poor people were supposed to sell to the rich everything they collected for a predetermined sum. As a result, a poor man would spend his whole life traveling back and forth on a scrawny horse, hungry and in rags. It was especially difficult in the fall and winter. He would be frozen through, wet to the marrow of his bones. If he had the good fortune to spend the night with a kindhearted peasant, then he could get warm and even get fed, but if the peasant was meanspirited, then the poor man wouldn't get across the threshold and would spend the night in the field or the woods. With that kind of hard life, he could never settle accounts with the rich man. He was always in debt to him. And his family was good and hungry. Meanwhile, the rich man kept saying that without his support, the poor man would have died of hunger a long time ago. That kind of life made poor people brutish and ill, and they died young.

So my father set out to establish a bank for these poor people. But the rich people in our shtetl wouldn't permit it, as they knew that if a poor man got money from a bank, then he wouldn't sell his goods to them cheaply. And as it is well-known that poor people can't compete with rich ones, my father expended a lot of energy, even traveling somewhere, before the bank was finally established. The poor people were off the hook; my father was pleased, and they were grateful.

My father had such a noble character that if somebody was in trouble, in or outside his family, he considered it his duty to help no matter what. Also he loved art. He acted in plays; in fact, nothing could be put on without his participation. As was customary among Jews at that time, all the plays were about Jewish history. Some of the most famous were *Khokhmes Shloyme*, which means "The Wisdom of Solomon," and *Mkhiras Yoysef*, "The Sale of Joseph."[5] There were many others.

The one thing he didn't like was his profession. The main reason was that it didn't pay enough to live on. But he was also exasperated by the slowness of some children. He would say, "When you teach a bright pupil, then you see the fruit of your labor right away, but when you teach (as he put it) a blockhead, then you repeat the same thing over and over to him without end, and he stares at you without comprehension like a sheep looking at a gate that's just been put up." He also often worked with pupils but didn't get paid for it. For most parents, tuition—*skhar-limud*—was the last thing they got around to paying. In such instances, Father would say that his trade was worse than a water carrier's, because if you didn't pay the water-carrier woman, then she wouldn't bring water, and another one wouldn't take over because the first one hadn't been paid. But if you don't pay the melamed, not only will he not send the pupil home, but a different melamed will be happy to take him, even for free, because everybody needs pupils. Many times he tried to abandon his trade and take up something else, but he didn't have any other profession, and no money to learn one, so he couldn't think of anything. He did have rich relatives on my mother's side, but the rich don't like to help their own families any more than they like to help strangers. And so, with a broken heart, he would go back to his heder, though he hated the profession and kept saying the same thing about the rich people in the shtetl, his contemporaries: "How am I worse than they are? I was a better student, and I know as much as they do. But they live in comfort, and

---

5   Both were well-known *purimshpils*—plays staged for the Purim holiday.

I have to be a pauper, saddled with this heder, treading water forever"—that was the expression that he used. This is what I know about my father. Since he was poor, my life was hard also.

I remember my own life from the age of four, and before that my knowledge comes from my mother's stories. Although I remember my mother as quiet and pensive, she did sing, but only when she was rocking a baby, and her songs were always sad and made me feel like crying. She told me that when I was little I was often sick but was also very clever. When I grew up a bit, I became sensitive and observant; nothing escaped me. We lived in a small wooden house with small windows, but our neighborhood was considered the center of town. The house was Grandfather's. He had two houses on his plot of land; he lived in one, and we lived in the other. But he spent all his time at our house, much more than at his own. When Grandfather died—that is, my father's father—I was only four, so I barely remember him. He was a tall man, very kind and very intelligent. When some of our Jews had arguments, he was always invited to help sort things out. He loved and respected my mother very much. When she complained to him about something, he was very sweet and comforted her. At that time I didn't understand her sorrow, but later I understood everything.

I remember how he died, suddenly, in the middle of doing something. He was buried with great honors: there was a *hesped* [eulogy—MB], which is like a public memorial. All the shops, Jewish and Russian, were closed, and nobody worked that day. The shtetl looked dead; everybody went to the funeral. I've been told that even babies were taken from their cradles. Every man considered it an honor to carry his body.

His line of our family was highly respected but poor. Grandpa was a rabbi of the eighteenth generation. His forebears were the Syrkin family from Chechersk.[6] They were important people, very learned. There were no businessmen or craftsmen among them. My mother's family was better known, because in the first place the family was large, and second, everyone was in business, so almost all of them were rich.[7] My mother was the youngest of the sisters and the poorest, but nobody thought of helping her except for my grandfather, when he was still alive. When I was around five, my mother got sick. The cause of her illness was the following. I have a brother Abram. When he was

---

6   Doba-Mera's father, Izrail', was the first to bear the family name Gurevich. As the second son in his own family, he was eligible for the draft, so his birth was ascribed to a different family.

7   It is curious that Doba-Mera nowhere mentions the name of her mother or maternal grandfather.

a child, he was sickly. The cause of his illness was an unsuccessful bris—Jews have this ritual to circumcise newborn boys.[8] After his circumcision he started getting abscesses, which afflicted him until his third birthday. He couldn't sit or walk, and he kept screaming from the pain. And since we lived in a shtetl in the middle of nowhere, there was nobody to treat him. At last Mother took him to a doctor in Surazh, which was practically her hometown. She was born in the village of Ulazovichi, seven kilometers away. They traveled in a wagon, and she held the little boy on her lap. When they arrived and she started to climb out of the wagon, she lost her balance because her leg had gone to sleep, and she fell and hit her side hard against the axle. But since she never had time to think about herself, she didn't go for help. As a result of this injury, she damaged her lungs and became seriously ill. But poverty did not permit her to look after herself and get medical attention.

So for that reason, from the age of five I became a big girl and started helping Mother do everything around the house. I understood the difficulty of my situation and my family's situation. People talked to me the way they would talk to a grownup. I had no time to play outside with the other children. At that time there were two of us children in the family. There had been another brother before Abram, but he got sick and died. When I turned six, my father started teaching me to read and write together with the pupils in his heder. According to my father's stories I was very bright and quickly understood everything he introduced. When he talked with his friends, he always regretted that I was a girl and not a boy. "That," he used to say, "is because a boy needs a good mind to continue his education, which is crucial to him as an adult, whereas a girl can get along without an education, particularly a Jewish one." Of course, by the standards of his time he was right, because a woman from a poor background needed a profession, a craft, as they used to say, in order to make a living for herself. Of course, in well-to-do circles there were families that educated women to become, for example, teachers, doctors, midwives and doctors' assistants, and so forth. And women like that could probably earn enough to support themselves, but no matter how much we wanted something like that, no matter how smart we were, we couldn't have it, because we were Jews and, to make matters worse, poor ones.

Let me take a moment to explain to you why poor people and Jews couldn't study like everyone else. When Russia was a capitalist country—that is, when

---

8   The memoirs are written for her descendants, who she assumed would be completely assimilated and would not even know that Jews practice circumcision.

it was ruled by Nicholas II—he was called "the monarch of all Russia," and in secret "Bloody Nicholas." He and his ministers kept issuing new, repressive laws against poor people in general and especially against minorities, in particular Jews. Jews aspired to an education, but the Ministry of Education wouldn't let them into schools, saying that Jews would take over, because there would be more educated Jews than Russians, and the Jews would crowd the Russians out. For that reason they decreed that schools could be only 7 percent Jewish and institutions of higher education only 5 percent, so that only the rich could get in and the poor couldn't even dream of it.

Thus I had no childhood, only years during which I was a child. In the circumstances in which I grew up, nobody treated me like a child. They talked to me the way they'd talk to a grownup. This is easy to explain. First poverty, and second, my mother's illness. In addition, my father was always busy, so he talked to me the way he talked to all his pupils: he asked me if I had learned the lesson that had been assigned, or he sent me off to eat or to sleep. Conversations more or less like that went on until I was around eight or maybe eleven. At the same time, he used to really praise me to his friends. He taught me himself, as I said, and gave me an education in Yiddish, Russian, and Hebrew. He himself taught me the real Talmud, which was absolutely off-limits to girls, and the history of the Jews in Hebrew. This "higher learning," as he called it, was given only to boys, but since I was bright, and there was no other kind of education he could give me, he didn't, as he said, have the heart to tear me away from my studies. He understood perfectly well that an education in the Talmud wouldn't do anything for my future. But he nevertheless decided that this was better than no education at all, because he loved education and used to say about me: "Let her study; it won't hurt her in her future life; it won't weigh her down." Also, we didn't have a boy who could study. My brother Abram was still little, so my father taught me the way he would teach a boy. But I felt alone among the boys in the class and was always happy when it was time to eat or when the school day ended.

In the first year of my studies I was already learning the *Humash*—that is, the Pentateuch—which gives the history of the Jews from the creation of the world until their conquest of Palestine. Because our shtetl was small, everybody quickly found out that Velia—that was my father's name—had a gifted daughter and that she was a better student than the boys. Men sometimes came to hear me recite. They would praise me highly for my intelligence, and then my father would be ecstatic with happiness. He would send me outside and himself praise me with delight to his visitors. There were even parents who sent their sons to study with my father on the condition that they were placed in my group. Sometimes my father would have me help weak students learn the assignment, and I was always happy to do this, because I understood how hard it was for him to cope with them on his own. But when I explained things to them and they didn't catch on, I was astonished. Why didn't they understand? Because I understood a new idea right away.

In general I had an easy time with my studies, but still there were things in the Talmud that were beyond my childish understanding. And why children's heads were filled with such things, I to this day don't understand. During lessons I used to ask over and over about the confusing parts, but instead of explaining, my father gave answers of the type "When you grow up, you'll see," or "It's not good to talk about this," or "It's not permitted to question this." For example, I was confused about how the creation of the world began. It just didn't fit into my little head, and I was not satisfied with the explanations that I was getting. As I remember it now, my father was astonished at my questions, because others didn't have them. Almost always he used to respond that God forbade such questions. Even now, as an old woman, I can't understand why my wanting to understand would make God angry.

So it was that between the ages of five and ten my life was almost monotonous: a whole day at heder, and for whatever time was left I helped my mother around the house, because she was ill. Since my mother felt bad that I couldn't play with girls my age, she sometimes let me go out. In school I was with boys and outside with girls. I had a lot of girlfriends, because their parents liked them to play with me. That was because, first, we were considered an honorable family, and I was a good student. Second, the girls liked and respected me because I studied well and did everything around the house. People used to call me a little child with a grownup head. On the Sabbath I used to play with my girlfriends, and they had dolls—true, they made the dolls themselves out of rags, but I was seized by envy. My childish heart would speak, and, going home, I'd think that I would also make a doll. But if the boys caught sight of it, they would grab the doll and show it to each other and make fun of me. So then I started hiding my dolls from them. To tell the truth, I didn't particularly like playing with dolls, because since I spent most of my time with boys, I naturally got accustomed to their games. For example, indoors they played feathers, and outside they played knucklebones, hide and seek, and other games. I could hit the target as well as they could. In those days other girls absolutely couldn't do this.

Another reason my girlfriends liked me was that I was always cheerful and could sing well. I knew a lot of songs: sometimes my mother sang, and my father sang on the holidays. We also had a neighbor who lived across the entryway from us.[9] He had a big family. They fixed galoshes, and that's what they lived on. On winter evenings when they worked, they would sing old Jewish and Russian folksongs. I learned from them and sang those songs too, so when I got together with my girlfriends, everybody would shout in unison that they wanted to learn new games or to sing, and from that moment on everybody was in a good mood.

When I was ten or eleven, three of us—me, Fania Rubinchik, and Dasha Blanter—decided to teach poor Jewish girls to read and write. Why Jewish? Because there was a school for Russians, and Jews weren't accepted there. And so on Saturday, almost all the little girls from our shtetl would gather at the Rubinchiks', and we taught them to read and write and gave them homework.[10] But one day a strange-looking vagrant came to the door, and everyone shouted that he was a police spy sent to check on what we were doing. In addition, it was impossible for everyone to meet as a group, because for things like that you got arrested and sentenced. So we all hid until the vagrant left. After that, we stopped our lessons, because our elders threatened us as well. Of course, we felt awful about it; we badly wanted all the girls in our shtetl to know how to read and write.[11]

We dressed very poorly. The only dress I owned wouldn't be new but sewn from something else, as a result of which my winter dress was always light-colored and my summer dress was always dark. To make sure that it would be clean for the Sabbath or a holiday, the night before I would wash it, then put it on again in the morning. And that's how I would wear my only dress until it got worn down to threads. But my shoes were always in good shape, even if

---

9 The entryway (*seni*) was the part of a wooden hut between the porch (really a stoop) and the living quarters of the house. Generally, this part of the house was unheated.
10 As Jewish law forbids writing on the Sabbath, the little girls were certainly violating it.
11 Aleksandra Brushtein (1884–1968) describes a similar case in the novel *Doroga ukhodit v dal'* [The road leads into the distance] (Moscow: Gosudarstvennoe izdatel'stvo detskoi literatury, 1957), based on her childhood in Vilna (Vilnius). The heroine of that book, Sashen'ka, along with her girlfriends, decides to bring her weaker classmates "up to speed." Since they do this without the knowledge and approval of the school administration, when the affair comes to light they are almost expelled from the institute (a privileged school in Vilna). In those years, any gathering, even of children or adolescents, needed official approval, as young people, especially if Jewish, were automatically suspected of working for the revolution.

they were ugly. That's because my father's pupils always included the children of well-off shoemakers, and they made us shoes instead of paying tuition. Of course, the shoes were not made as conscientiously as shoes for people who ordered them—that is, those who paid cash—but we were still happy to have them. I remember that I once had shoes made that buttoned. They were called "Hungarians," and for some reason both of them were for the same foot, so the two sets of buttons looked like they were chasing each other and I was embarrassed to wear them. People made fun of me on the street, saying that I had started a new fashion, and I was ashamed to walk in them during the day, but in since I had no others, I had no choice. At the same time I didn't envy other girls who had good things. For one thing, there weren't many people who had the money to dress their children well. On the contrary, there were children who were dressed even worse than I was.

At that time, when I was ten or eleven, my studies underwent a small change, which I remember very well. A teacher of secular subjects appeared in our shtetl. His name was Dodin. He taught all subjects and himself studied as an extern, as was the custom in those days. He began to give lessons to both boys and girls. A lot of parents sent their children to him, and my father sent me too, because he thought that I could combine this with the heder. So every morning I would study with a group of four or five other children. The teacher praised me to my father, and the time I spent with him didn't affect my studies at the heder. My father wanted me to be special in comparison with other children. He had a colleague who knew Hebrew well, including all the grammar rules, and my father sent me to his group too.[12] His name was Khazanov, and he was a very intelligent and educated man.[13]

---

12 Doba-Mera's father's desire to teach his daughter Hebrew, which at the time was not taught in heder as a separate subject, points to his sympathies with the Jewish Enlightenment and Jewish nationalism, possibly even Zionism. The rise of Jewish nationalism and Zionism in Russia during the second half of the 1890s and the early 1900s led to the flourishing of a set of "improved" or "reformed" heders (the *heder mekutan*). A "reformed" heder was similar to a normal primary school and taught not only Jewish tradition but also contemporary Hebrew, Hebrew literature, Jewish history, Russian, and, in a superficial way, some general subjects (Zvi Halevi, *Jewish Schools under Czarism and Communism* [New York: Springer, 1976], 110–15). Apparently, "Father's colleague" was a teacher at a reformed heder. The original text uses the Soviet term for Hebrew—"ancient Jewish"—not the Jewish or Hebrew language.

13 The reference appears to be to Leib Khazanov. His granddaughter Liuba, thriving at age ninety, describes him in her memoirs:

> Grandfather was a melamed—a teacher in a heder, a Jewish primary school. Grandmother also worked as she could—she was a seamstress, an amazingly hard worker. I didn't know

I studied with him in the evenings—also in a group of four or five children, mostly boys, of whom nobody is alive now except Epshtein. All of them were older than me. I was the only girl, but there too I studied well. Before a lot of time had passed I had learned to write and read and recite poems in Hebrew.

The only thing I had trouble with was spelling with the letter ѣ.[14] This was a letter that used to be part of the Russian alphabet, and you had to memorize all the words in which it was found. I didn't sleep at night, memorizing those words: *beg* (running), *begun* (a runner), *beglianka* (a runaway), all words in which the ѣ appears instead of "e." And after all words that ended in a consonant you had to put a ъ. After the revolution, there immediately appeared posters saying, "Down with the letter ѣ." That's when people started writing "e" instead and stopped using the hard sign ъ.[15]

But I loved poetry, especially Pushkin, especially "Who Is He?" and "Storm Clouds"[16] and many others, and I loved Krylov's fables and I loved to read books, although there was never any time.

I wasn't fated to study for long. My mother got weaker and weaker; she couldn't be restored to health, and we couldn't give her the special foods that she needed.[17] Even though she came from a large family and almost everyone [in it] lived well, nobody wanted to help. One time she was persuaded to go

---

> Grandfather; he died before the revolution of 1917, but I remember Grandmother well, as our family also lived in Khotimsk from 1921 to 1932. Grandmother lived until 1941, when she and our other relatives were murdered by the Germans together with all the Jews in the shtetl.
>
> From the memoirs of my cousin Alik (Aleksandr) Khazanov, the son of my uncle Mendel, I learned that Grandfather was a man of prodigious talents—knowledgeable in the Talmud, and a mathematician and a chess player. He was not Orthodox; he knew Yiddish literature and folklore. Of course, my cousin knew about this from his father's stories.

Liubov' Solomonovna Khazanova, "Recollections of the Khazanov Family," manuscript. Collection of Michael Beizer, received from Israel Kheyfets, a resident of Emanuel and the great-great-grandson of Leib Khazanov.

14 Apparently it was considered good form to criticize the letters ѣ and ъ.
15 Memorizing a long list of words featuring the letter ѣ was a nightmare for Russian schoolchildren. The spelling reform that did away with this letter, as well as the hard sign at the end of all words ending in a consonant, was promulgated by the Provisional Government. It was made into law by the Bolsheviks in December 1917 and brought into practice in print and administrative usage in 1918.
16 "Mchat'sia tuchki"—she gets the title slightly wrong.
17 Here and elsewhere, Doba-Mera assumes that good food is the most important element of treatment for an illness. The Russian implies that she could not eat on her own.

to the doctor in Klintsy. She had a rich brother there, Izrail´ Medvedev, but he didn't even let her into their living area. He made her sleep on a hard trunk in a cold hallway—that's the kind of help they gave to their sick, poor sister. The doctor didn't consider her illness serious and told her to see him once more, but since there was no place to stay she didn't make the trip again, despite the fact that his treatment made her feel better. Mother understood that her days were numbered. Very often she would focus her gaze on me and say, "What will become of you when I am gone?" How terrible for a child to hear such words from her mother! You can't wish such a thing on your worst enemy. Her condition kept getting worse, and I spent more and more time doing housework. I made dinner and baked black bread and white bread. Since I was small and couldn't reach the oven, my father built me a little platform, and when I cooked I put it in front of the oven, and when I was finished I put it away. When the neighbors came to visit Mama, she would praise my bread, saying that as a mother, she had a lot of grief over me when I was little but wouldn't live to get joy from me.[18]

Then came the fall of 1903, the month of Heshvan, around November. Mother could not get out of bed. These were the last days of her life. With horror I now remember what I lived through then. It was painful to see her torments, to watch her take leave of her life and her small children. Up until the last minutes of her life she understood her and our position. I remember the wise, golden words she spoke before her death. I listened to her with great attention, clenching my teeth so as not to sob, so as not to let drop a single word. I stood at her bedside, and it seemed to me that she wasn't dying but going away for a while. There were three of us children. I was eleven, the oldest. Then there was my brother Abram, a pale thin boy, and a year-old baby, not yet weaned. I will write down a little of what she said, because it would be impossible to write all of it. She told our father that after her death he would need to be a mother to us as well as a father, and that he should protect us from harm when he took another wife, because she knew he would remarry; he was only thirty-eight years old. To me she said these words:

> You yourself are still little, and you will have two little ones to bring up.
> As long as I was alive, even though I was bedridden, you weren't orphans;

---

18 What is meant is that Doba-Mera was often sick in early childhood, causing her mother great anguish, and that her mother didn't hope to live until the joy that would come from her daughter's marriage and the birth of grandchildren.

you didn't have a stepmother. But when I die, the three of you will be little orphans, and you will be the oldest. Care for them like a mother, make sure they aren't hungry and cold. Know that your father is a good person, but he is a man. He has suffered with a sick wife, and he will have to get married, because he is only thirty-eight. His relationship to you will get worse, because his wife will demand it, and although he won't be happy about it, he will not want to damage his relationship with her. You will have to give in to her in everything without saying a word, because nobody is going to stand up for you, and if she gets angry at you, the littler children will suffer the most. If she offends you in word or deed, then cry in secret so that nobody hears, because if they do they will tell her, and things will only get worse for all of you. From the moment I close my eyes, the whole world will reject you. Because only happy children are loved.

She said many other valuable things, but as I already said, you can't write down everything. Then blood spurted out of her throat, spraying her and the bedding, and Father and I started to wipe it up, and she, pale, let her weak head fall back on the pillow and closed her eyes. Red marks appeared on her sunken cheeks, and she fell asleep forever. And then I gave into my tears and my incurable grief. This happened at dawn, in the fall, in 1903. I don't remember the date in Russian, but in Jewish it was the twenty-sixth day of the month of Heshvan. I fell sobbing onto her bed and stayed there until the neighbors came and tore me away, saying: "Enough crying. Save your tears, you'll have enough use for them without a mother." Father also cried a lot and, hugging and kissing us, said: "You are my poor orphans, what will I do with you?" Abram, my brother, stood there terrified. He didn't know what he should be doing. We were taken away to Papa's sister Lyfsha's; she lived right near us, that's Senia Brisker's mother.[19] Her husband was a very bad man. We were afraid of him, and he didn't like us. In general he didn't like anybody, only himself, and because of that he lived well his whole life, and now he is sixty-five and hale and hearty. Anyway, when they brought us to him, he gave us a hostile look. But I didn't care then. I couldn't even think about him. When they got ready to carry Mother out according to Jewish tradition, we were called to say farewell to her, and that was when I understood that we no longer had a mother; she would never return to us. Father accompanied her to the cemetery, and we remained at home.

---

19 Doba-Mera probably means Briskin. Michael Beizer remembers a relative by the name of Senia Briskin, from childhood. He died in Israel around 2000.

From that moment the very foundation of my life changed. I grew in understanding. People talked to me the way they would talk to a grownup. My baby brother called me "Mama," which cost me many tears.

To come to terms with my past life, I will give a little description of my father's family, particularly his sister Lyfsha and her husband, Alter. My parents never told me anything bad about them. That was because my mother was such a submissive woman and such a believer in her God. She believed that God would punish those who offended other people, and that if Lyfsha sinned all her life, then she would pay for her bad deeds later, but when "later" would be I didn't understand then and still don't.[20] Father had a good character. His temper flared sometimes, but he quickly forgot offenses and spoke to those who offended him as though nothing had ever happened.

I was told about my father's relationship with his family after Mother died. As I already said, everybody considered me a grownup, and because of that our Khotimsk acquaintances told me about it, and as I grew up I could see the truth of it on my own. Father grew up without his real mother. There were three children: that is, his two older sisters—Galka, who was thirteen, and Sora, who was eleven—and my father, who was eight. Since he was male, he was considered the oldest and the protector, although in fact he couldn't help them in any way. Their stepmother treated them very badly, and since Grandpa was not only an unassertive old man but a very pious one to boot, he couldn't influence his wife to improve the situation of his children. Father and Aunt Khaia-Sora—that's Adol′f's mother—were taken to live with their aunt in the shtetl of Vetka, not far from Gomel′, and there they stayed until they were grown.[21] Galka, the mother of Gershel Budianskii, somehow suffered through with the stepmother. No sooner had she grown up than they married her off. She had a bad time of it, and she died before reaching old age. With his new wife, Grandpa had two more daughters, Lyfsha and Gesia. They lived in poverty, like the majority of Jews in our shtetl, and that only exacerbated the stepmother's relationship to children who weren't her own, the more so in that she was an aggressive woman, with a hard, bad character. Stepmothers usually teach their children to hate their stepbrothers and sisters, finding all sorts of flaws in them. This is what happened in Father's family. For that reason, as

---

20 The memoirs were written in the most "Soviet" period of Doba-Mera's life. For that reason, she uses a class analysis of social life and emphasizes atheism, which she abandoned during the war years.
21 Doba-Mera has in mind Adol′f Gusakov, who later married her husband Meilakh's sister, Sima Medvedev.

soon as Grandpa died, the hatred in the family intensified because of an insignificant inheritance. The stepmother's treatment of Father was harsh, even cruel. I don't want to get into it, since none of them are alive any more. Even though my father's stepmother was my mother's own sister, she had no problems harassing my father and even my mother, and she didn't like us children. As a result of their hard lives, nobody in the family, including Father, lived into old age. Only later did I understand the family's role in the premature deaths of my parents. I'm not saying this just because I'm the daughter: all our family and friends in Khotimsk and many other relatives used to say when they saw me, "They drove your parents to an early grave." You'd think, why remember this, it's not going to bring them back. But for some reason I absolutely wanted to write about this, even if only a little. Also this [discord] played a big role in my life, as I will describe later. So as I was saying, at that point Alter came on the scene, the husband of our father's sister Lyfsha. He was a *yeshiva-bokher*, a student in the advanced Jewish religious school. He had an excellent Jewish education, and even in Russian he knew a lot. He was like everybody who lived and studied at someone else's expense. People like that were deadbeats and slackers. They always looked for a rich bride or, if all else failed, the kind of wife who would earn money and feed them, the deadbeats, all their lives. Sholem Aleichem has written a lot about people of this sort. They were good for nothing and weren't prepared to do any kind of work. My uncle Alter belonged to this group. In addition, he was by nature cruel, uncommunicative, and very mean. He was very egotistical and was always convinced that everybody was for some reason obligated to him. In general he lived the kind of life in which he never gave anybody a glass of cold water, and he didn't even give his old mother enough to eat. At the same time, he really looked after himself. Now he's already in his sixties, and he's still ruddy, full of energy, and in good health. People like that always age well. So this person no sooner appeared among us than he started taking command of everything and everybody. He took advantage of his mother-in-law's—that is, my step-grandmother's—bad attitude toward my father. To make matters worse, before his marriage he had been promised a big dowry, almost mountains of gold, but once he married he found the opposite. It's true, there was a store that sold clay pots, but its inventory was at that time worth almost nothing, and it was burdened with debts that probably exceeded its value by several times.

Alter's first move was to take away my father's seat in the synagogue. Of course, the way I look at things, both now and earlier, and in the opinion of many people, there's nothing remarkable about that: "Big deal. So he took away your seat in the synagogue. You can go to the synagogue without a seat, or you can not bother going at all." But that's how people think now—back then it was completely different. As I already wrote, my father rarely used his seat, because he preferred to be with poor people, so he usually walked about the synagogue. When his brother-in-law Alter first appeared, my father seated him in his own place, as a brother and a guest. Alter responded by taking that seat over from the very first day. When my father would arrive and try to take his seat, Alter would try not to notice him, pretending that he was deep in prayer, or he would simply not let Father sit down. Finally he declared that the seat was part of his, Alter's, dowry, and Papa retreated quietly, so people wouldn't hear. For my father, this was a huge blow. Most important, the seat had belonged to his own father, whom he loved very much and respected for his education. To make matters worse, people started to make fun of him, saying that he couldn't stand up for what was his. A lot of people invited him to sit in their seats, but he didn't want to take over the places of other people. At that time, according to Jewish tradition, seats in the synagogue went from father to son, not to a daughter, because women didn't pray together with men. From the moment that his brother-in-law took over his synagogue seat, my father hung out with the paupers, partly because he always enjoyed talking with them and partly because he had no other place to sit. At that time to pray in the synagogue without a seat was the same as going someplace you weren't wanted. He didn't have the money to buy another seat, and in any case he would have been ashamed to do that in front of his acquaintances.

In this way Alter entered our lives. Knowing this one thing is enough to understand the way his mind worked. When I grew up, I came across a novel in Yiddish called *Der shvartser yungerman*. It describes how a son-in-law was taken into a home, and how little by little he took control of everything and everyone and sent everyone to their graves, so nobody would disturb him.[22] The hero of this book reminded me a lot of Alter, and I shed a lot of tears over it. This book clearly showed me Alter's true face and his ugly deeds and

---

22 Doba-Mera recollects the book *Ha-Ne'ehavim veha-ne'imim; oder, Der shvartser yingermantshik* (The Beloved and the Pleasant, or the Black Young Man) by Jacob Dineson [Yankev Dinezon], which was first published in 1877 and became the first long and sentimental Yiddish novel and the first Yiddish bestseller. See Jeremy Dauber, "Dinezon Yankev," in *The YIVO Encyclopedia of Jews in Eastern Europe* (New Haven: Yale University Press, 2008), 1:408–9. The novel is about the adventures of a young couple in love, who could not unite because of the machinations of an evil ("black") little man. It is interesting that Doba-Mera remembers the name of the evil man more than the adventures. Thanks to Mikhail Krutikov for the information.

the role that he played in our family. Even so, to this day he doesn't consider himself guilty. After he took over the seat in the synagogue, he decided to dispense with my parents and take over the entire inheritance, even though it was small. He relied on help from my step-grandmother, who had no love for my father as a stepson, and met no resistance on the part of my parents, whose honorable nature he abused.

Grandpa had two little houses. They stood next to each other, with their windows facing the street. In one, which was bigger, Grandpa lived with his family—that is, Grandpa, Grandma [in fact, Step-Grandma—MB], and their daughters Lyfsha and Gesia. And we lived in the little one. While he was still alive, Grandpa divided the houses between his family and ours and divided the land that belonged to them as well. Since our house was very small, as I already wrote, and Father could do a little carpentry, he began to build another house in the yard, a bit bigger. He bought another house in the village that was slated to be torn down and started building. This happened in the winter, because labor was cheaper in the winter but more expensive in the summer because of field work. Father loved that kind of work, but he was busy, and it was too much for any one person. But the time came when they carted this house over. Grandma was the first to run outside, followed by her sons-in-law and daughters, and they started raining curses down on my father. Never will I forget his frightened face. "What do you want from me? I'm building on my own plot, and staying clear of the boundary, according to regulations." My mother was too scared to leave the house. That's how they began to build our "nine-by-three *arshin* palace."[23] People from the shtetl came to try to persuade that family to stop harassing Father. The spiritual rabbi,[24] who at that time was considered a respectable figure among Jews, also came to have a chat with them, but in vain. Alter screamed at my father that everything belonged to him, Alter, and that if my father wanted to build, let him buy the land and build. My father was ready to sell the logs he bought for the house, but our Jews came down hard on him, accusing him of weakness: "You gave away your seat in the synagogue,

---

23 Nine arshins are the equivalent of 21 feet or 6.4 meters.
24 Between 1857 and 1917, a rabbi in the Russian Empire had to be elected by the community in accordance with instructions from the government. Such a rabbi was called a *kazennyi ravvin* (official or crown rabbi). Official rabbis served the authorities as a tool to influence and control Jewish communities. These rabbis had to know Russian, but their knowledge of Jewish law was often limited. Therefore communities employed, along with a crown rabbi, a second, traditionally oriented rabbi, a *dukhovnyi ravvin* (spiritual rabbi), whom the believers trusted.

and now you're going to give away a house you already bought, and soon you and your family will get thrown out of your house. You see what kind of appetite they have: everything for themselves, nothing for you. Start building." So Father started building. As is well known, wooden houses are built on a foundation. People who are rich use stone, and poor people use wood. First they dig a foundation pit, and then they put down posts, and over that they put logs. This was happening in the winter, and where we lived, frosts begin in November, and by the middle of the winter the land is frozen very far down, so that even the water in wells freezes over. The construction of our house started exactly at that time, and the days were short; it was impossible to dig with a shovel. They had to use axes and a crowbar, so that after a day's work they hadn't laid down a single post. Alter made use of this. As soon as the workmen had left, he poured water into the pit, and by morning it had frozen, and they had to start over from the beginning, and nobody could figure out what to do. Father was in despair. Mother, in tears, pleaded with him to give it all up, explaining that we were poor, and everything we had was pawned, and he was paying people for nothing. A lot of money had gone into it, and a lot of heartache, and nothing had been done.

Then Father decided to keep watch. This was no simple matter, from four in the afternoon until eight in the morning. For sixteen hours he had to stand in thin clothes in a heavy frost, then work with children for an entire day. But this was his only means of escaping his impossible situation. The family itself, that cheat Alter excepted, for all their bad character and hatred for Father, would not have behaved that way, because they were afraid of what people would say. But in Alter's presence they danced to his tune. It's not honorable of me to write about this, but I hope that nobody will find out.[25] Some time passed, and then Lyfsha, as the devoted wife, adopted his evil character to the point that they were one and the same. She never gave money to beggars, behavior that people in the shtetl considered shameful. They lived isolated lives, like snakes—that's what people called them. And nobody liked them; people even hated them.

If a stranger were to read these lines, that person would likely be surprised that I give so much significance to these things. But as a witness to them, I can't remember them without horror. Is it even possible to describe all the evil Alter did to my parents? A man decided to take everything for himself and get rid of everyone who stood in his way. And he was successful. Every day he thought of new forms of harassment, so that in the end Father decided to move away, find

---

25 This is, of course, a misleading statement. Doba-Mera wrote for her descendants.

work, and then call for his family. And he did move away, but without money, without skills, with a sick wife, he was forced to return. In the meantime, Alter started a war against the old woman and Aunt Gesia. He sent Grandma off to live with her older daughter and himself started to harass Aunt Gesia, often beating her. More than once she ran to us to hide from his attacks, until he sent her off to Klintsy to her sister. There a tragedy happened—Aunt Bluma, Gesia's sister, died, and her husband, now my uncle Belkin, was left a wealthy widower with two children. Aunt Gesia had only just turned eighteen. At that point Alter put his brains to work, flew off to Klintsy, and began insisting that Aunt Gesia be married off to Belkin. Her protests that she didn't want to marry an old man, her sister's widower, were useless. Then Alter got Grandma to help by threatening that he would bring her back to live with him and not let Aunt Gesia past the threshold. He got what he wanted. Aunt Gesia was married off to Belkin, and Alter killed two birds with one stone: he got rid of two heirs, Grandma and Auntie, and assured himself of future aid from his rich relative Gesia. And so it worked, because he was used to living off other people.

Despite all the suffering his stepsisters caused him, Father forgave them everything, he felt sorry for them and truly loved them, as an honorable brother should. When Father learned that Auntie was being married off against her will, he felt very bad even though he had a good relationship with Uncle.

In the end both my parents left the earth before their time, and we, little ones, were total orphans. Can I even describe all that we suffered growing up? Everywhere and to everybody we were unwanted strangers. Nobody wanted to think about us, and they, too, were not dear to my heart. But Aunt Gesia changed after her marriage and became a good person, sensitive and responsive. Apparently this happened because Uncle himself was a good man with a warm heart; he liked to help people and in addition was well-to-do. Maybe that influenced her, and she took me to live with her, and I went, like a little hunted animal with nowhere to turn. Her attitude toward me was often caring, and I would have been fine had it not been for the interference of her mother, who was afraid that my presence would diminish the amount of help going to Lyfsha. I gradually became accustomed to my aunt and came to the conclusion that her former bad relationship with my father had not been her fault. An inexperienced, provincial girl, she was under the influence of an evil old woman, her mother, and controlled by Alter, who was threatening to throw her out onto the street. I long ago forgave her everything, but Lyfsha and Alter I did not forgive and will not. . . I am sure that if they could, they would harm us even now. It's enough to say that Alter's own old mother lived with them, and he didn't give her food to eat. The neighbors fed her out of pity. They were indifferent even to their own children. They didn't want to give them an education, although thanks to their interest in learning, some of them got one anyway.... I could write a lot about their cruelty toward us and toward their own children, who have no good memories of them. These people, Alter and his wife Lyfsha ... who started behaving just like him, were cruel people; they were despots then, are despots now, and will be despots to the end of their days. Twenty-two years of Soviet power have failed to turn them around, from which it can be concluded that they will remain that way....

Truly, I became grownup right away—not in years, not in height, but in understanding. My life changed immediately. I left my studies, because I had to take care of my family. I stopped going to heder and learning Hebrew. For a while I stopped studying Russian also, but then I took it up again, and only when I was with a book could I forget about all that gnawed away at me.

Then my father's friends started urging him to get married, saying that it would be easier for me with an older woman in the house. I, of course, got the picture right away and was very afraid of a new mother. Father, it is true, didn't want a second wife, especially since he had his own sorry experience living through eight years of cruelty from his stepmother. Finally they got through to him, and he decided to marry not someone he liked but someone who would treat us well, as he was convinced that a second wife like my mother he wouldn't find under any circumstances. He was presented with the mother of my sister Meita, and five months later a new mother came to live with us.[26]

I remember it as though it were today. Before she arrived, our rooms were fixed up. Mama's furniture was thrown out, and new furniture was brought in. Every step taken in the house matched my mother's predictions, which made me suffer all the more. Then came a day before Passover, when Father left to get married and bring his new wife home. Since we were little, he asked his aunt to stay with us during that time. There we were, we three and a little boy from the country we had living with us, and Fania Brushtein and Doba Gusakova spent nights with us. Because of all the bustle I caught cold and coughed so hard that I couldn't walk. They arrived at night. I look: into the house comes a lame, ugly, middle-aged woman with a mean expression, and I was coughing so hard that I didn't say hello. But she, paying no attention to my cough, unceremoniously began counting the children. There were three of us and three others: that came

---

26 Doba-Mera means her stepsister, the daughter of her father and stepmother. Meita was killed by the Nazis in 1941.

to six. Then she asked Father: "You said you had three children, why are there six?" Father comforted her, saying that three weren't ours, but she didn't calm down until morning came and they went home.

Once again my life changed: I had to satisfy a new mother and defend my little brothers. Little by little, Father started talking to me less often. As I found out later, this happened because she scolded him for being too soft with us, because she believed we were bad children, and he was more attentive to us than to her. Father became gloomy and irritable. He understood that he had made a mistake, that he had taken on someone who was not a wife, a mother, or a housekeeper. She didn't want to do anything. Father ran errands for her, although in those days it wasn't considered acceptable for men to go to the market, and everybody laughed at him. Instead of becoming easier, my position became a lot worse, and my heart ached for myself, for my father, and for the little children. I had been accustomed to feeding the children whenever they wanted to eat, but now they ate when she said they could. Of course, her position wasn't the best, because we were poor, but this wasn't the children's fault. I assume she knew that we were poor before she married. She started locking up the food. My God! From whom? We had a tiny child, and she should have been the one looking after him, not hiding things so that I couldn't feed him.

A family named Leitosh lived in our shtetl, relatives of my mother. It was a good family. They had four daughters, the youngest of whom was my age. They were well-off. This family was my only comfort. When I was with them I shared my grief. Once, soon after the appearance of our new mother, I accidentally found a letter addressed to her from her sister Khona, written, apparently, in response to a letter from our stepmother in which she complained about us. Let me give some pieces of advice from Khona: Watch that you hide everything from the children, or there will be nothing left for you. Take charge of them. Let them know that you are in control." And she immediately put this [advice] into effect. Here's another good episode. Her mother came to visit—a tall, thin woman who looked like a witch—and immediately started fighting with us helpless children. I remember well how on Friday evening Father came home from the synagogue, and we sat down to eat. Before dinner the baby wanted to eat, but the old woman wouldn't let him have anything before everyone else did, and by the time we sat down at the table, he had fallen asleep hungry. As he was sleeping in my arms, I tried to wake him up, but he didn't respond. Then I left the table and carried him to bed, but since my youthful heart was full of grief and I felt sorry for the baby, going to sleep without his supper, tears flowed from my eyes. Returning to the table, I no longer wanted any food, because I was filled with suffering, but no matter how hard I tried to wipe away my tears, the old woman saw them and pounced on me, saying that I deserved to be whipped daily, that my father lived and breathed for us, and started demanding that he punish us. Tormented, Father answered that we were punished enough by being orphans. My brother Abram, who had turned nine, got frightened and crawled under the table, and I went to the baby, and hugging his sleeping body I cried the whole night through, asking everything sacred to help me and asking my departed mother to take us to her, because without her we had no life.

The next day, the Sabbath, I found a moment when Father was alone and spoke to him. For a long time I had wanted to talk with him, to find out why he was silent in the face of all the torment we were being put through, and at this point my cup was overflowing. And so I spoke and didn't understand how I had the intelligence to do it.

Wise people say that a person's intelligence appears with his suffering. The more suffering, the more intelligence. I, however, would prefer less intelligence and less suffering. I asked my father if his silence in the face of the torment unleashed by our stepmother and her mother was going to continue for a long time. His answer was that he couldn't raise our mother from the grave, that whoever he married would be a stranger to us, and that he did not intend to start a fight with his wife and make himself the butt of people's jokes because of it. I understood the whole intractable nature of our position.

It's good that our father never beat us, although they tried to get him to do that. He had fallen under a double blow. In the presence of our stepmother he hardly spoke to us, fearing to arouse her anger against us. Once our little brother cut his head with a piece of glass. I got very frightened and called Father. When Father saw the little boy covered in blood, he scooped him up and cried, "My poor orphan, when will your torments be over?" And we all cried in response to these touching words, and even more because Papa loved us. And so our life passed, one day worse than the next.[27]

I had to give up my Russian lessons, because my new mother announced that she didn't have the money to pay for them. It didn't help that my father said I was talented. She categorically refused and fired the teacher. An older girl who gave Russian lessons, from a family named Malkin, offered to teach me for free when she heard that my stepmother had refused to pay. But my stepmother wouldn't let me learn my lessons. I had to study in the attic or in

---

27 In passages like this, the memoirs imitate the style of Russian socialist realist writers.

the yard behind the wood pile, and every time I had to think up a new spot so that she wouldn't find me. I was supplied with textbooks, but once I needed one that I couldn't get. I will never forget it, it was Ilovaiskii's *Russian History*. Father bought it for me on the sly, and I kept hiding it. One day my stepmother found it and screamed at Father: why was he wasting money on me? What, he wants an educated daughter? What's the problem if she becomes a seamstress? This book played a huge role in my life. My studies came to an end because of it. Even now I remember the incident with pain in my heart, because it destroyed my life. If I had received an education, my life would have meant more, and it would have been easier for me to live and raise my children.

The summer of 1904. Everything was the same. Father taught his pupils, our new mother imposed her own rules on the household. We children stuck close to one another. We swallowed our tears in silence.

One evening, when I had cried my fill, I went to sleep without supper, which happened often. I was sleeping, and I dreamed that my mother, as if she were alive, appeared before me and said: "Don't cry. When I was alive, I kept saying to you, 'Look out for yourself and for the children.' You see, even Father can't help you." I remember this dream as though it were happening now. Before me stood my living mother, and I cried out in my sleep, "Mama!" I wanted to throw myself into her arms, and at that point I woke up. My father was standing next to me. Apparently I had awakened him with my cry. Choking from my tears, I couldn't answer his question about what I had dreamed. My stepmother was tossing and turning in her bed, unhappy that by day and night there was no rest from us. My only comfort was to visit Mother's grave and have a good cry. After that my heart felt lighter.

My father had a cousin, Yoshe-Iche (Iosif) Slutsker. He sometimes came to intercede for us. A few times he tried to have a good talk with our stepmother. He tried to pick fights with her, too, because he loved us very much. But nothing worked. I didn't dare even to approach the cupboard, even though it had been brought to our house by my mother. It was hard to believe that such a pitiful-looking woman had control over everybody, but that is precisely what was happening.

When my mother was alive, I never envied anybody, and after her death I envied only those who had a mother. I was very angry at those children who didn't obey their mothers and caused them to worry. If I had a mother, I would have pity on her and would obey her in everything.

In the summer of 1904, my stepmother went to visit her relatives in the city of Starodub, where she complained to them that we weren't letting her live. They then decided to take Father there to live with them, leaving us on our own in Khotimsk. Father went, leaving us in the care of a tenant family who would live in our house. I already wrote that our house was divided into three parts: a bedroom, a main room, and a kitchen. The tenants, naturally, took over the bedroom, and they ate in the main room where we, according to the agreement, were supposed to sleep. Since they had a big family and little children, and he, the head of the family, was a butcher, they got up early and went to bed late and we had no time to sleep. They took over all the rooms. We had a very hard time, especially the littlest brother, who cried nonstop. It was indescribable.

Fall came, ushering in the Jewish holidays, and we were still alone. At that time a woman arrived from my mother's village and said that my grandfather—my mother's father, he was then still alive—had invited me to visit them for the holidays. I could get there on the same cart that had brought her. Since there was nobody to leave my little brother with, I took him, and I left Abram to the winds of fate. It is terrible to remember all this.

I arrived at Grandpa's, in the village. Grandpa was very old and lived with his son and his son's family. His son was Uncle Iakov Medvedev. Grandpa hadn't been told about Mother's death, and I was warned not to speak about it. (As I later understood, the family was afraid that Grandpa would give us material help.) Nobody expected us; apparently the idea of us moving in with Grandfather belonged to that woman, who knew that we were having a hard time on our own. It turned out that we arrived at the wrong time. Since they were very observant, and the village didn't have a synagogue, for the big holidays they went to pray in a bigger settlement or a nearby shtetl. Since they all left for the holidays and had to take us along with them, we created additional work. So we celebrated the New Year, and the Yom Kippur fast was coming soon. It got cold. We were lightly dressed. They had to send us home, but there wasn't an excuse. And what did home mean? Who did we have at home? Who was waiting for us? And then a wagon came through on its way to Klintsy, and my uncle, without giving it much thought, put us on it, not even thinking to cover us with a blanket. And it was already fall.

In Klintsy lived my mother's brother, Izrail′ Medvedev. (That's the grandpa of Ven′ka and Dus′ka and Osia and Liova.)[28] At that time he was rich. I wasn't asked if I wanted to go there, and I absolutely didn't want to go because of the way he had treated his older sister, my mother. My mother used to say

---

28 Osia (Iosif), Izrail′ Medvedev's grandson, married Ida, his third cousin, the younger daughter of Doba-Mera, after World War II. It was Ida who gave Michael Beizer his grandmother's memoirs. They had a daughter Zhenia and a son Venia. See Beizer's introduction to this book.

that he was very miserly and didn't like his poor relations. But I wasn't asked, and that's where they sent us. They reasoned that from Klintsy it would be easy to find a wagon to take us back home, since a lot of goods traveled from Klintsy to Khotimsk. We left Grandfather's village in the evening. While we were on the road, a cold rain began to fall. We traveled all night, were soaked and shivering; the child was crying from cold. In the morning we arrived.

The peasant driver brought us to my uncle's house. Since he didn't know Uncle, he himself opened the gate and drove into the yard. Uncle himself came out and asked in a saccharine way, "Who are these children you have brought me?" "They are the orphans of your younger sister Rokhl'—that's the name that peasants used to refer to my mother. "So why did you bring them to me?" asked Uncle. "You, Ven'iaminovich," said the driver, "take them off the wagon, warm them up and feed them—they are hungry and wet—then ask your questions. Look, the poor little ones are frozen stiff."[29] "They were visiting Grandpa, you understand," he went on, "and the folks there couldn't figure out how to get them to Khotimsk, and I was on my way here, so Iankel' asked me. 'Take them,' he said, 'to Klintsy. From there it will be easier from them to get home.' So I took them. The night was wet and cold and I covered them with my robe, but the poor things froze anyway." And Uncle stood by the door and stroked his beard and said, addressing the driver by name: "I have nowhere to put them, but they have an aunt here, their father's sister. They don't live very far; take them there." He had in mind Aunt Gesia, about whom I wasn't even thinking at the time. I knew only that she didn't like my parents and that she had gotten married recently. If that rich man, my mother's own brother, with his mansion and his small family, didn't even walk up to us to ask if we were hungry, acted worse than someone who was a complete stranger, then what could I expect from my aunt, my father's stepsister, who didn't like him? I remember this now and bitter tears flow. Can one imagine a worse situation? I was in a strange, unknown city, with a small child on my hands and without a cent. Poorly dressed, in the rain, in the fall, not needed by anybody, abandoned by everyone. Who put me in this frightening, impossible situation? Our new mother: she took away our father, who was supposed to take the place of our mother for us.

The driver, distressed by the way Uncle was treating us, took off his hat and pleaded with him, saying, "Ven'iaminovich! Fear God! Tomorrow is your

---

29 The use of the patronymic (Ven'iaminovich) alone, without a first name, in conjunction with the intimate rather than the formal word for "you" (this doesn't appear in the translation) was typical of the behavior of uneducated people among themselves. This form of address was considered respectful.

big Jewish fast. The Day of Judgment. How are you going to fast before God if you chase away these little orphans, your sister's children?" But Uncle stood immovable and said to the driver, "Here's something for vodka; take them to their aunt." The angry driver threw the money back at him, took the address, and left the yard leading the horse by the reins. He continued along the main road, still fuming and muttering to himself. Suddenly he stopped the horse, turned to us and said, "And if they don't take you there, what am I going to do with you then?" At this my little brother started to cry loudly, and the driver, confused, as though he were guilty, said, "Don't cry, I'll think of something; I won't leave you on the street. That rich uncle was frightened by poor orphans, but I'm poor myself and poor people don't frighten me."

And so we reached the house of Aunt Gesia Belkina. There was nobody home but a servant. She was a Jewish servant, young and dark-complexioned. The driver explained to her that we were her mistress's relatives and that we were frozen and hungry orphans, and she was happy to take us in. The driver was happy that we were finally off his hands. He left quickly. Zlata—that was the cook's name—fed us and warmed us up, as attentive as though we were her family. Then Aunt, Uncle, and our step-grandmother appeared. There were questions: where had we come from, what was going on. Auntie seemed happy to see us. Uncle was very warm toward my little brother, since he was both beautiful and exceptionally smart. After our meeting with Uncle Izrail′ all this seemed to me like a magic dream, and I was afraid I would wake up and find it gone.

After hearing my story about how we turned up at her house, my aunt said that it was good that we traveled through Klintsy and that she had wanted to see us. About our visit to Uncle Izrail′ I said nothing, afraid that she would also chase us away. Auntie tenderly washed us, dressed us in dry clothes, and put us to bed. She said that there was no point in rushing, and that when the weather improved and a good cart turned up, then she would send us home. At this time my uncle Izrail′, knowing how he had treated us and afraid that I would tell my aunt, and she had an important position, so he was afraid this would affect his business, decided to preempt me by subterfuge and avoid Aunt Gesia's wrath. On the evening of that very day he sent his wife and daughter, ostensibly to visit, but at the same time to find out if Auntie was angry at him for his wicked deed. Not suspecting anything, Auntie told them about our arrival and praised us, my little brother particularly, and right away came to where I was and said, "Your aunt has come with her daughter.

Come out and say hello, they want to see you." But I refused, saying that I was embarrassed to meet them because I was poorly dressed.

Not suspecting anything, satisfied with my answer, Auntie left. And they left. The next morning, Uncle himself came with his saccharine smile, as I saw from the doorway of my room. Auntie greeted him and asked, "Would you like to see the children of your departed sister?" He answered grandly, "Of course!" Auntie came into my room and said, "Your Uncle Izrail′ came specially to see you. Come out and say hello to him." I answered that I wouldn't go and gave the same excuse as before. Auntie began to insist, saying that this was no stranger and that there was nothing to be embarrassed about. "After all, he's your mother's brother, and if he sees that you are poorly dressed, he will buy clothes for you, because he is rich." What could I do? Anger my aunt? Why? Unable to find a way out of my dilemma, I started to cry. To Auntie's question as to why I wouldn't go out and meet my uncle I could not find an answer, because I was afraid to disclose to her what he had done. But Auntie understood that it was useless to insist and that some deep mystery was afoot.

She decided to leave me in peace. Going out to Uncle, she announced that for some reason I was crying and didn't want to greet him, then added that for some reason I was ashamed of my clothes.

When Uncle left, Auntie came right back to me and said, "I can see that you are hiding something important from me. Don't be afraid and tell me everything." Not finding any other way of justifying my behavior, I had to tell the truth. When I had finished my story, I saw that my fear of being chased away from Auntie's house had no basis. The more I told, the more serious she grew. Agitation made the color of her face change. Angry and in tears, she went to Grandmother and said, "So he loves me only because I am rich. If I were in their situation, he wouldn't let me past the threshold. From this moment, they are strangers to me." And turning to me, she added tenderly, "I understand. You were afraid to tell me because you thought I might do the same thing. I will not forgive him for what he did to you until he repents." Comforting me, she said, "Don't cry. You'll grow up, you'll get married, you'll live better than his children, and you will forget about this."

Auntie kept her word. For a long time she had nothing to do with him, although the next day she went to see his daughter, Kheva Lokshina, in her store and told her off, saying that nobody knows what will happen to him tomorrow and that *erev Yom Kippur* people do many good deeds to make up for their sins, while Kheva and her family feared neither God nor people and chased hungry orphans out onto the street, and these orphans might in time live better than they do.

From that moment, Auntie became dear to me. With my childish head I understood that she had become a different person, and that her former relationship to me had changed. We had found the only person in the world who had pity on us and sheltered us, although not for long.

Soon we were sent home. And who and what awaited us there? For there was nobody there. We were sent off well, with a good cart, well-dressed, with food and money for the journey. Since Mother's death this was the first time that anyone had treated me tenderly. You can imagine how I felt then, if even now my tears are making it hard for me to write.

Little in the way of consolation awaited me at home, but we were happy to be back in our own little corner. As I've already written, the family of the butcher Dobin was living in our house. He felt sorry for us, but he also took advantage. For example, since they often gave my brothers something to eat, I didn't want to be in their debt and helped them with the housework. Gradually this became a habit, and so it happened that at only twelve years of age I took care of both my own brothers and a large family of strangers.

A cold winter set in. Our tenants would come home late from the slaughterhouse or from a trip, and we slept in the main room, which had no doors, so that the cold from the street was carried right to us. Because of this my little brother came down with diphtheria, and I, still so young, had to take care of him. I made him breathe steam from a special little samovar and stayed under the sheet with him. I did everything the doctor said to save his life. When he fell asleep, I would run to my mother's grave and complain, crying, about our life and about how we all had been abandoned. During this time I sent my brother Abram to live with a poor, kind old woman, while I took care of the little one myself and did not catch his illness from him.

In that way the winter, then Passover, went by. During that time I got a letter from Father saying that at the insistence of our new mother's family he had decided to sell the house and take us back, and that we would all live with her family. Despite my youth I saw that here we had one stepmother, and there we'd face a whole crowd of them. I objected and insisted that if we had to leave, then better we go to a different city, as otherwise they would eat us alive. However there was no other city where somebody we knew could help our father find work.

I remember as though it were yesterday that I wrote Father a letter and he heard me. I'll give a summary of my letter. I reminded him that we were unhappy little orphans, deprived of a mother by cruel fate, and that because of our stepmother we had also lost our father, who left us alone, without sustenance, for such a prolonged period, and that now he wanted to deprive us of our own little corner and bring us to a stepmother who would quickly disperse us to the four corners of the earth with a bag over our shoulders. I wasn't defending myself then, because I could always find a place. But my brothers, the poor little things! I felt so sorry for them. In short, as spring came around, my father and stepmother returned home, and Father revived his heder. This was the spring of 1905.

When the summer came, my brother Abram fell ill with scarlet fever, and the doctor said that the other children had to leave the house. My little brother and I were sent to stay with the poor old woman who had taken in Abram during my younger brother's illness. We hadn't lived there long when the old woman became seriously ill and we had to find another place to go. At that time there appeared a *balegole* (a Jewish cart-driver) from the shtetl of Shumiachi, where my mother's brother Abram lived.[30] People said that he was kind, because when he found out that Mother was ill, he took her to live with him and she stayed there for two months. She returned home almost healthy and praised him and his family. Father decided to send us to him. Uncle didn't live in Shumiachi itself but somewhere nearby, in the village of Krasnopol′, on a gentry estate. He was either an agent or a manager there (at the time, I didn't understand these things), or maybe he had a lease.

We were greeted warmly. I was afraid to tell the truth about why we had come, lest they send us back. I said we had come to visit. I counted on staying for the period of Abram's illness, approximately a month. The manor house was old and large with a broken balcony—a real, broken-down noble estate. A big orchard. Far from the village. At that time Uncle Izrail′ was also visiting them, that very same uncle who had not let us into his house, along with Aunt Rokha, their daughter Sarra, and son Azriel′. They got more attention than we did, but at the time things like that didn't matter to me.

After a month we returned home. There I found Abram in a dangerous condition. He had caught cold, and he had an inflammation of the kidneys. When I caught sight of him, I got scared: he was so fat—that is, blown up—that it's hard to describe. He was so happy to see me that he said, "I nearly died. Of course, it would have been better if I had, except I felt sorry for you." And we both cried.

---

30 Balegole is a Yiddish term for "cart driver," derived from בעל עגלה (*baal agala*, cart owner [Hebrew]).

Father came in and said that it was still forbidden for us to be near him and that he had made us a place to stay in the attic. Father gave Abram baths, and he recovered.

Then Father decided to send me to Klintsy to Aunt Gesia Belkina. He said to me, "Maybe they will send you to study. They are rich. What would it cost them to educate you, and make you into somebody?" Father put together some clothes for me and even a winter coat, because he was convinced that I would stay there for a long time. When I arrived uninvited, I didn't calm down for a long time because I kept remembering how my brothers cried when I left. Grandmother was not happy to see me. She was afraid that her other daughter, Lyfsha, would get less attention because of me.[31]

Auntie didn't have any time to think about me, and I hung around without occupation. At that time a female relative came from Novozybkov and said to me, "What are you doing hanging around here without occupation? You're not little any more. Your mother's brother lives in Novozybkov. He's a kind man, he lives well, and he'll set you up somewhere."

And so I went to stay with Isaak Medvedev. They were a big family, three daughters and three sons. They greeted me decently, the children liked me, but Uncle was either always very busy or didn't want to ask why I had come. Then I spoke up for myself and said that I wanted an education. Uncle answered that I was poor, so an education was out of the question. However, if the idea was to learn a trade, then absolutely he would help. In their yard was a big stocking workshop, with a lot of girls sitting at round machines. I often walked up to the window, and I liked to watch them working cheerfully and singing various songs. I started asking them to let me join. They responded that the machines didn't belong to them, that there was a boss and that my uncle should talk to him. The boss was someone by the name of Neishtadt, who lived right there. When I asked my uncle, he said those girls were depraved, that they sang bad songs. Later I discovered that they were singing revolutionary songs, forbidden by the government. Eventually I came to understand that this wasn't the problem—he simply didn't want to take that burden on. I had to return to Klintsy, to Aunt Gesia. In Novozybkov, of course, nobody shed tears over my departure and here nobody was pleased to have me back, because everywhere I was an unnecessary burden. Despite my limited life experience I understood this very well.

---

31 Lyfsha, Alter's wife, living in Khotimsk.

I returned to my aunt in Klintsy at the beginning of August. The happy children were bustling with preparations for their studies—that is, for the beginning of the school year. Standing at the gate, I watched them enviously. At that time, the only things I yearned for were lessons and a book bag. Next door to Auntie lived Minkin. He had a daughter Liza who was around my age. She was studying in a gymnasium and was about to start fifth grade. We soon became acquainted, and I understood that she knew about the same amount as I did. Delighted by my discovery, I told her that I also wanted to study at the gymnasium. Just hearing the word aroused in me an incomprehensible happiness. How much more was I drawn to the idea of studying there like other children, carrying a satchel on my back, wearing a uniform, and, most important, becoming educated. I began to study intensely, to go over all I knew, which was quite a lot.

When the time came for the entrance examinations, I started asking how to apply, whom to ask. Then Liza burst out laughing and said with irony, "People like you don't get past the gymnasium door." The hurt has remained in my heart forever. I didn't understand at the time why she was making such fun of me. And I decided to go to the gymnasium myself and find out what was going on. When I got there, the doorman informed me that there would be no examinations for externs (that's what they called people who studied on their own), and that no more Jews would be allowed in the gymnasium, as their quota had already been filled.

I returned home. I didn't want to broach the subject with my aunt, but I asked Grandma to ask my aunt and uncle if they would let me study. But Grandma was already worried that Auntie would squander all her assets on me, so she was firm and decisive. "Get this education idea out of your head," she said. "You're not Minkin's daughter, and you're not a Belkin. You are a poor orphan, and Auntie has decided to send you to apprentice with a seamstress so you can earn your own bread." At this point I understood that my studies were over, and being in no condition to keep back my tears, I fled from the room.

It happened just as Grandma said. A few days later I was sent to apprentice with the seamstress Sosha. She had almost a dozen girl pupils and two master apprentices, a junior one and a senior one. Nobody bothered to teach us anything. She herself was a widow and the sole support of two sons and a daughter. The older one was a coppersmith who worked for an artisan, the younger one was a clerk in a store, and the daughter studied at the gymnasium. We pupils were supposed to prepare the irons and do all the housework, including washing floors and running errands. But we weren't taught to sew.

The senior apprentice was good to us and without the boss's knowledge would let us sew something and showed us how. But she soon left, and only one apprentice remained, a Klintsy girl by the name of Riva Krasnovskaia.[32] We didn't like her. She sucked up to the boss and ratted on us.

When I had adjusted to my new circumstances and made the acquaintance of the boss's daughter, I asked her what it was like to study and how she got into the gymnasium. This question was giving me no peace. She explained to me that our tsar and his officials didn't like Jews and made life hard for them in every way. Educational institutions had Jewish quotas of only 5 to 10 percent. Only the rich got in. They could even get nothing but Cs on the entrance exams and then study poorly; no matter what, they wouldn't be expelled. And she herself got in because her mama sews for free for the head of the gymnasium. At this point I understood why Minkin's daughter was laughing at me—because her father was a wealthy fish warehouser. I saw that education would forever be off-limits to me, as there was no way I could ever be wealthy, and even if I do have wealthy relatives, they don't even want to think about me. Even if they met me they would try not to notice me, so I wouldn't compromise them by my presence. I never remember my relatives, and my children know practically nothing about them. Why should they know? They would only regret having relatives like that.

September passed. The month of October began. Strikes broke out.[33] Some people came to see us and said, "Comrades! The workers in all the factories of our city are on strike. We, as tailors, must also stop working as a sign of solidarity with them. And so we ask you to stop working and go home. Our demands are economic. When they are satisfied, we will get back to work." We didn't understand what was going on. "But we're just learning," we said. "We're not getting paid; in fact, we're paying to learn. What should we do?" They told us that we were the same as workers, since with the help of those

---

32 Apparently this is the same Krasnovskaia who is later seen in the Bolshevik underground.
33 October 1905 was an important stage in the Russian Revolution of 1905–1907. A workers' strike began in Moscow and seized the whole country. In mid-October more than two million workers were on strike in various industries. This general political strike, particularly the one among railroad workers, forced Nicholas II into concessions. The manifesto of October 17 granted civil liberties: personal immunity, and freedom of conscience, speech, assembly, and association. However, the revolutionary parties were not satisfied with what they had obtained, so they set out on a path of armed struggle with the goal of overthrowing the regime. The spontaneous public response to both the manifesto and the broad participation of Jews in antigovernment activities led to massive, bloody, anti-Jewish pogroms throughout the Pale of Settlement.

who were learning, a boss could get away without hiring workers. Hearing that answer, we solemnly set off for home.

We liked the whole scene. The streets were full of people. Everyone was dressed in their best clothes. People were walking in crowds, talking loudly, arguing. There were demonstrations. [Talk about] the autocracy, Bloody Nicholas. I don't remember anything, but wherever the crowd was, I was with it. I wanted to understand this new thing, find out what those words meant. But I was embarrassed to ask strangers, and my friends didn't know.

At that time we were told that the trains weren't running. All the railway workers were on strike. The trains stayed put for a long time, around a month.

I was rarely home. I went to the workshop, and there was Krasnovskaia, working away. I asked her why she wasn't following the orders of the strike committee to stop work. The committee had announced that anybody who worked during the strike would be called a *shtreykbrekher*. What a *shtreykbrekher* was I had no idea, but it sounded threatening. Krasnovskaia answered that those snot-nosed boys didn't lay down the law for her. Naming them one by one, she said derisively: "Some lawgivers! Barefoot and in rags! They'll all be put in jail, and then they'll find out what real hardship is like."

I didn't understand what they would be put in jail for, but from that moment I started to loathe Riva and like the people she was attacking, and when I ran into them I was the first to say hello. I liked the fact that they used words that not everybody understood.

A few days went by, but the strike continued. People said that to make it happen, somebody came from Surazh who used the name Taras Bul´ba.[34] This was a big, stocky fellow. Nobody knew his real name, and if there were people who knew it, they kept it a secret so he wouldn't be arrested. I learned that there were demonstrations every day at the Old Believer cemetery. The old, dilapidated cemetery was not far from the former Baryshnikov Factory, and workers from all over the city gathered there. At that time the place was called Bald Hill.

During the strike I saw myself as completely grownup: after all, the order not to work included me! Walking around town, I caught sight of people distributing printed sheets. They would appear, look around, throw down a packet, and move on as if nothing had happened. I grabbed a leaflet and read, holding my breath. The heading was: "Workers of the World, Unite!" In the text, it said that the strike had already been going on for some time. Almost all

---

34 Taras Bul´ba is the hero of the novella of the same name by Nikolai Gogol´. He was the ataman of the Zaporozhskii Cossacks during a period of anti-Polish rebellion.

of Russia was on strike with us. Factory owners and bosses were rejecting our demands, threatening us with police action. Come together at such and such an hour on Bald Hill. Signature: The Workers' Committee.

When I finished reading the leaflet, I decided to have a look at the demonstration. But how could I leave the house without permission? I knew I couldn't get permission, so I went without it. I quietly scouted out where the place was, and even though I was feeling timid because I was so young and going to a place where grownups went, I did go. Never before had I seen so many people. One man was standing on a stump and speaking. That was Taras Bul´ba himself, the leader of the strike. He was speaking from the heart, cursing the tsar and those in power, cursing the factory owners and bosses. He said that the owners were threatening to call out the police and declare a lockout (that means to use their rules to fire all the workers and not allow them to work). Let them go hungry, and then they will work for any wage. At this point many other people started speaking. Some proposed holding out longer, and others declared that they were already going hungry, that it was time to get back to work, as it's difficult for a poor man to fight with a rich one. Others said that the committee would help those in need. At that moment people started screaming: "Police! Cossacks!"

Indeed, many mounted and foot police and Cossacks had appeared. Many people got frightened and ran off, but the majority stayed in place. At first I ran, but then I wanted to see what the Cossacks and police would do. Before this I had not been afraid of the police; in fact, I admired their uniforms. I stood by a gate from where I could see Bald Hill, which was much higher than the surrounding streets. The police surrounded the crowd of strikers, and Cossacks on horseback rode into the center of the crowd. They took the speakers and some more people, then started dispersing the crowd with whips. They dispersed them and rode off. But the crowd reassembled and started yelling, "Let's go and free our comrades!" And the crowd of a few thousand people rushed toward the police. The police at that time were headquartered where the Soviet police are now, on Bol´shaia Street, now called Karl Liebknecht Street. There they stopped and started choosing who would go inside to ask for the release of the arrested comrades, when the police chief himself came out and said, "Disperse, or we'll shoot." The crowd responded, "We're not moving until you release our comrades, even if you kill us." This continued for a long time, but the arrested men were released, and the crowd dispersed.

The strike was, of course, undermined. The arrests began, and whoever wasn't arrested got fired, and a worker who had been fired couldn't find a new job anywhere. The factory owners hired Cossack guards. The Cossacks were ferocious and couldn't speak Russian.[35] At the time they served as the blind tools of the factory owners in their fight against the workers.

After that, I became afraid of the police. If I came across a street patrolman, I was afraid of his gaze. As for Cossacks, if I so much as saw one on the street, I wouldn't walk along that street for a long time. Terrible things were said about the Cossacks. People said that workers met secretly at the Zabegaevka Cemetery, and the Cossacks surrounded them, and whoever they caught, they tied to the tails of their horses. Then they set the horses to galloping, and the man tied to the tail couldn't keep up, so he was dragged along the cobblestones. When he was good and bloodied, they brought him to the police, where there were interrogations and more beatings. The police chief at the time was a certain Pavlovskii. People said that his brother was in service to the tsar. Those who participated in the underground workers' organization at that time remember Pavlovskii, if they survived. It didn't matter if you were a party member or not, if you fell into the hands of the police chief, he would either beat you to death or leave you a cripple for the rest of your life. He would beat people in such a way that there were no marks on the body—he'd seize someone by the hair and drag him, or beat him on his sides, over his heart, on his stomach, and he liked to do all this himself. The mere mention of his name made people tremble.

How did he get his hands on people who had no relationship to the Party? It happened because a lot of bosses handed over workers they didn't like, and this was enough to destroy a person for the rest of his life.

The factory owners organized themselves into a Union of True Russians.[36] People called them the "Black Hundreds," and the whole thing looked a lot like contemporary Nazism. Their goal was to crush the workers' movement and build up ethnic hatred, in particular by fanning the flames of anti-Semitism [underlined in the original—MB]. They advocated crushing the Jews as a dangerous anti-Russian element. Russian poverty is caused by Jews. High prices in the marketplace are caused by Jews, because Jews are rich and buy a lot, and nothing is left for Russians. They invited all workers to join this organization. Those who joined were hired, and those who didn't were fired as instigators.

---

35 To disperse demonstrations, the government frequently made use of Cossack regiments composed of national minorities: Buriats, Kalmyks, Tatars, Mordvins, Caucasian mountain peoples, and others for whom Russian was a second language.

36 In 1905 the Union of True Russians (*Soiuz istinno russkikh*) was the organization of the Black Hundreds (V. P. Meshcherskii and others). It merged with the Union of the Russian Folk (*Soiuz russkogo naroda*).

Party workers were also called instigators. They could denounce any worker they didn't like to the police, and even if they didn't, [they could ensure that] a person with a record like that wouldn't get a job anywhere, and he would go hungry until he left his hometown for somewhere far off where he would take any job under any conditions.

There were traitors even among artisans and tailors. The most famous was Moisei Aronov. He ran a sewing shop; he drove his workers very hard but didn't like to pay them. A worker would ask and ask to be paid for his labor, and when he couldn't stand it anymore, he would say that if he wasn't paid for the time he had worked, he would stop working because he didn't have anything to live on. So as not to pay his workers, Aronov handed them over to Chief Pavlovskii. In addition, there were the tailors Falia Gultkin and Davidovich. They eavesdropped on the conversations of their workers and conveyed the contents to Pavlovskii. Many people suffered at their hands, people like Perlin (who died young) and many others. That is what I saw during my time in Klintsy, when I worked as a pupil for the seamstress Sosha.

It was October 1905. As always in our region, there was rain and frost, but nights were dark. You couldn't see a thing. The morning of October 17, when I set off for work, the streets were unusually lively. People who saw people they knew kissed them or shook hands, congratulating them on something. At first I thought it was some kind of Russian holiday like Easter, that Christ had risen, that the priests had once again thought up a way to increase their flocks. Then I saw that even Jews were congratulating each other. I was very intrigued by that, especially when I heard the word *stution*. As soon as I got to the workshop, I started telling everyone about it. And one of the girls said that her sister was in the Party and that she had said that the tsar had gotten frightened by the strikes—particularly the railroad strike that had been going on for about a month, when Russian life came to a halt—and had issued a *manifesto*. This was called a *constitution*. It meant freedom of speech, freedom of assembly, and some additional benefits for the people. She immediately added, "This could make things worse! Particularly for us Jews." In the evening, when I came home, everybody already knew. As I was walking along the streets, all the store windows had placards on them congratulating people on the granting of a constitution and giving detailed explanations of what a constitution was.

For Jews, the joy was short-lived. Jews became worried and started whispering to one another that the Black Hundreds were getting ready for some kind of action, and that more and more often anti-Semites and rabble-rousers were heard directing slogans at us of the type "Just wait and we'll show you your constitution." One evening during this period, as I was walking home, a group of Old Believers emerged from a house. They were lighting their way with small torches. A lively conversation had been taking place among them, which apparently they hadn't concluded. From what they were saying, I understood that they were coming from a meeting at which an important decision had been proposed and adopted.

When I got home, I told everyone about this. My uncle got angry at me, saying that because of people like me, innocent Jews would suffer. Of course, I got very frightened. What might that mean? I, a thirteen-year-old girl, was responsible for some kind of suffering I couldn't understand. I looked for Uncle's clerk, thinking that he would understand me better and explain what was happening. He took me aside and said that the tsar had taken his constitution back, and that since Jewish youth were against the tsar, the government was organizing pogroms against the Jews. When I asked what I had to do with this, he explained that all Jewish workers were being blamed, and I was a Jewish worker.

This explanation I understood, but why was it necessary to beat up and kill Jews if their children were, as he put it, "instigators"? Because Russian workers also took part in strikes. Hadn't there been a strike of railroad workers and workers of other factories where they didn't hire Jews? Why didn't anyone riot against them? The clerk answered that, first, because the tsar is Russian and, second, because Jews are aliens and have no right to interfere here and establish their own rules. Of course, I was dissatisfied with this answer and often thought that something else was hidden here, but what, I didn't know.

It was October 21. I remember as though it were today. A Friday. The Russians were having some kind of a holiday.[37] As usual, it was market day. Because of that, a lot of peasant wagons had driven in. They had driven all night. There were more wagons than people. People were saying that in other cities, anti-Jewish pogroms had already occurred on October 19 and 20. In Klintsy the Jews were already afraid to go outside, but those who sold at the marketplace nonetheless decided to open their shops. When they arrived, they found yellow crosses drawn on their doors in yellow, at the same time as Russian shops had white ones. That was so people would know which stores to loot. It turned out that the police had been preparing for this event.

---

37 Social convention at that time made hardly any distinction between Russians and Ukrainians and, to an even lesser degree, Russians and Belorussians. In Klintsy, located near the current borders of Russia, Ukraine, and Belarus, "Russians" could be any of the above.

They were helped by the Union of True Russians, and in response to an order from the Black Hundreds, the shops had been marked off by Petr Petrovich Dolgov, then still a young man.

I was not allowed to go to work. Frightened, we stood at our windows and looked outside. Almost no Jews went out, even to go shopping on such a big market day, which was even called "Family Friday." At the same time, the streets were filled with Russians, mostly peasants from the villages. Suddenly we heard screaming. Oh, horror! It's terrible even to remember it now. The Black Hundreds marched down the street yelling, "Beat the Jews!"[38] At that point they started looting the shops. They dragged dough out of Podperzin's bakery and started trampling it with their feet. Things started to burn. Jews hid as best they could. Evening was already approaching, and we were still standing at the windows watching people carry and cart away goods they had robbed from Jews. Trembling, we awaited our turn. Suddenly someone knocked at the window. We looked, and it was our neighbor, the worker Kulakov, ordering us to close the shutters and leave the house, as it was dangerous for us to remain.

But we decided not to look for shelter with Russians. We went out into the yard, which was surrounded by Jewish houses, because there was nowhere for us to go. Uncle confidently announced that it was already late, that the pogromists had already done a lot of looting and would leave us alone. At that point there was a knock on the door and a lot of yelling: "Hey, everyone! This is Belkin's house! Let's raid it!" The doors flew open, and glass rained down from the windows. For some reason we all ran into the kitchen and from there into a little pantry, from which there was a passageway through the Kulakovs' fence. Kulakov was telling us to come. And taking advantage of the darkness and a ladder he gave us, we made our way over the fence and onto the decaying roof, wet from rain. We younger people quickly made it over, but Grandmother had a very hard time. She was old and frightened, and she already heard what the rioters were up to in the house. Horror overcame us all. They finished their looting and threw down a torch and it ignited, but the Russian neighbors put out the fire. When the first group of pogromists was gone, we went to see what they had done. The windows and doors were broken. Clothes, underwear, bedding—all was taken. The room was covered in feathers, like snow. In their fury, they had torn open pillows.

---

38 A young girl's secondhand accounts must be handled with care. Who exactly cried, "Beat the Jews," the Black Hundreds or the crowd? Did the police organize the pogrom? Doba-Mera could only have learned about this from someone else. However, one must not dismiss this testimony as obviously false.

Then, suddenly, the shouting started again. Another group was coming, and we again ran to our neighbor's. My little brother Davidka, who later died, burst into tears. Where would we live, what would we eat? Uncle put on Kulakov's hat, so nobody would know him, and walked up to the gate. There a policeman recognized him and said, "Hey, Belkin, you want a really good hiding place? Let's go to the police station. There are a lot of rich Jews there." That happened because the chief of police wanted to make some money and sent his men to rich Jews, who would pay him for hiding them. Uncle agreed, because Kulakov was afraid to keep us in his house too long. So we set off with the policeman to the station.

They took us to the police precinct. A lot of Jews were lying on the floor, most of them wealthy. Children were sleeping. Some grownups were praying, and others were crying and tearing their hair out. It was almost dark, with only a wick burning in the corner. We weren't allowed to go up to the window, apparently so that we couldn't see that the police were also taking part in the pogrom and wouldn't be able to remember the faces of those who were rioting.

Morning. Saturday. October 22.

A policeman came and announced that the pogrom was over and that we could safely go home. When we got outside, it was incredible. In the Pochetukha neighborhood, the entire wooded hill was full of peasant carts that were returning to the city for another riot. They had developed a taste for looting. But at this point the factory owners became frightened that they would also get looted. Because the Jews had already been sacked, so there was nothing left to take, the Russians were next. In response to a demand from the factory owners, a guard was placed on the bridge so as not to let peasants into the city. The peasants were met by city officials, together with a priest and religious banners. The priest said prayers and persuaded everyone to go home quietly. In the end he said that under no circumstances would anyone be allowed in the city. The pogromists stayed around the bridge until evening and returned home with nothing.

I understood that poor Jews were the ones who suffered most from pogroms, because a wealthy person could find a safer place to hide, and even if all his possessions were looted, his status as a wealthy man remained. Businesses would respect him, and he could get back in the saddle. In addition, he still had real estate that couldn't be carted away. He suffered from humiliation as a Jew, but his losses were soon forgotten, and he began living as before. But if a poor Jew had his possessions stolen, considering that he couldn't get a loan before, he certainly wouldn't be able to get one now, so he faced a life of destitution. When we got out onto the street, we learned that only two people had been killed, the old woman Shakhnovich and young Khazanov.[39] They treated Shakhnovich in the most beastly way, first cutting off her ears and then pouring kerosene on her and setting her on fire.

When we entered the house, there were neither windows nor doors. Even the wallpaper had been torn from the walls. Everything that could be taken away was gone, and everything else was broken to pieces and looked like a pile of scrap. We started trying to clean up, in order to somehow go on living there, because it was already autumn, cold and wet. Jews insisted that they be assigned policemen to do searches for stolen things. The police chief, of course, was bribed to make this happen. Of course, a lot of things were found, but in those cases Russians immediately declared, "If you go after your things, we'll go after your blood." This meant that they were promising a repeat pogrom— not, this time, with the goal of looting but with the goal of exterminating the Jews. Later we learned who had started the pogrom. It turned out that the entire Klintsy and Surazh districts had received orders to make the peasants from surrounding villages take part in the pogrom, and that the organizer was the very same chief of police in cahoots with the Black Hundreds. The police chief also participated by giving advice to the looters when they found it hard to break into a Jewish store. For example, near the church on Bol´shaia Street was Peselev's furniture store, with iron doors that wouldn't give. So the police chief ordered that a pood weight be hung on a rope and swung at the doors.[40] That's what they did, and the doors opened. Petr Petrovich Dolgov himself marked the Jewish shops and houses and led a group of pogromists. He also visited rich Jews in their homes and proposed that they put an icon with a lamp in their window, saying that this would keep them safe. If a Jew refused, then he right then and there would start looting in the owners' presence. Among their number was the Jew Malkin. Dolgov proposed that he put an icon with a lamp in his window, to which Malkin replied, "If the Jewish God has turned away from me, then I'm not going to seek defense from yours." This made Dolgov angry, and he sat down at the piano, played for a little bit, then smashed

---

39 Possibly related to Nakhum Shakhnovich, a native of Klintsy and a member of the Central Committee of the Zionist Organization and the Council of the Leningrad Jewish Religious Community from 1917 on. In 1926 he emigrated to British Palestine. By the young Khazanov, Doba-Mera apparently has in mind one of the three sons of the melamed Leib Khazanov: Zalman, Khaim, or Mendel. See Khazanova, "Vospominaniia o rode Khazanovykh."

40 A pood weighed 16.38 kilograms or 36.11 pounds.

it to pieces, while Malkin's family fled the house. So that in short is my description of the Jewish pogrom in Klintsy in 1905.

After the pogrom I, of course, had no clothes. Everything I had was taken by the thugs. The shop had also been looted, and the material for dresses that people had ordered had been carried off, so there was no work. At the same time, information that the Klintsy Black Hundreds were getting ready for another pogrom spread far and wide and reached my father. He wrote telling me to come home and sent me something to wear for the trip. So that's what I did. When I arrived, I learned that they had not suffered a pogrom, and neither had the surrounding shtetls. People explained that Belorussian peasants had not been organized by the Black Hundreds and, in addition, lived peacefully with Jews.

But the Jews nonetheless prepared for a pogrom and organized self-defense. People armed themselves with whips, as guns were not permitted.

And so I was living at home with my father and my little brothers. Our stepmother was not with us; she had gone home for the fall holidays and had, for some reason, still not returned. Apparently it was better for her at home without her stepchildren.

I took care of the house. For the time being, Papa could not find work for me anywhere. Seamstresses were ready to take me on for three years of training for twenty-five rubles. Father was ready to pay, but he didn't want to commit me for such a long stretch of time [or], as he put it, "sell the child for such a long stretch of time."

Time passed. The winter was severe. There was no snow, but it was extremely cold. Russian Christmas was approaching. Miners began returning to their villages for the holidays. They traveled home through our town, and we were afraid of a pogrom. In those years miners were ignorant wild men. They were terrible drunks. They were sent underground for long periods, and an effort was made to keep them isolated from other people, particularly from other workers, to keep them ignorant. This benefited the mine owners. Every day these miners would pass through our shtetl. In such cases Jews would bribe the police constable and the counterman (selling vodka) [so that he would close the shop—MB]. Not everybody was permitted to sell vodka, and Jews in particular were kept away.[41] When the miners would come through, the liquor

---

41 Many Jews abandoned the distillation business after 1861, when the system of taxation changed from a fixed sum to a percentage. Then in 1895–1898 the government took over the sale of alcoholic beverages, thus setting itself up as the source of alcoholism among peasants and workers.

store would be shut, and then there was no danger. A sober man would hardly dare to riot. But then rumors started to circulate that on "Red Sunday" (the Sunday before Christmas),[42] a lot of miners were going to arrive and there would absolutely be a Jewish pogrom. People started preparing for self-defense—including the fire brigade, among whose numbers were many Russian strongmen but also many anti-Semites.

A Jewish self-defense group came from the shtetl of Kostiukovichi, thirty-five versts from us.[43] There were around thirty people in it. All of them were armed with revolvers and Brownings. They were young and intelligent, some of them craftsmen, others day laborers. They came at night, and everybody found out about it immediately.

On Sunday morning the miners started to arrive. The Jews were afraid to open their shops. The miners started shouting for the shops to open, saying that they had to buy presents to bring home. Some people opened. Then they started to demand that the liquor store open, but that was not done. At that point the miners looted the Jewish iron shops, seized bits of iron and other heavy objects, anything that you could break a lock with, and headed for the liquor store. When they had broken into it and had enough wine to drink, they started looting the other shops. At this point something unexpected happened for the Jews. They had been counting on the fire brigade. Indeed, when the rioters broke into the liquor store, one of the firemen, a young and very brawny man named Shidorin, set his group against the rioters. At this point a Russian strongman, also a fireman, tripped him as if by accident. Shidorin fell, and the rioters killed him. That's when the Jews understood that the fire brigade would not defend them—quite the contrary. Then the newly arrived Jewish defense group rose up from across the street and started shooting into the crowd of rioters. They were scared by the shots and started leaving the shops.

At that time a student named Mogilevkin, a Russian, was in town for the holiday. His family lived by the market. According to rumor he was a democrat and against the tsar. He came out onto the front steps of a shop and started to give a speech to the miners. He tried to persuade them not to riot against the Jews, since they were people like everyone else, and that it was the government

---

42 The Russian Orthodox Church does not have a holiday called "Red Sunday." It is not clear what Doba-Mera meant. A novel written in 1916 (Iakub Braitsev, *Sredi bolot i lesov* [Minsk: Registr, 2013]), describes the Khotimsk pogrom, which began around January 4, 1916, prompted by the miners who had been fired. The novel mentions Shevel' Shifrin, murdered in the pogrom; the self-defense group from Kostiukovichi; and Prince Obolenskii.

43 One verst is the equivalent of 3,500 feet.

that wanted pogroms and was inciting the miners to bring them about. But the crowd didn't want to listen. Then, seeing that he wasn't going to dissuade them from a pogrom, he suggested that they loot the estate of Prince Obolenskii, which was not very far away and had a distillery attached to it.[44] "Why loot poor Jews when you won't get anything from them?" The rioters liked this idea, and they headed off to the prince's estate—not, of course, without breaking the windows of Jewish houses on their way. And the student Mogilevkin disappeared (he went into hiding) to avoid arrest.[45]

When the rioters broke into the estate and found out that the distillery vats were full of pure alcohol, they started drinking and took some of it home. The news that there was free alcohol quickly spread from village to village. People starting coming on sleighs with whatever vessels they could find. As they did this, they said that once they got their liquor, they would start looting the Jews.

Then the fun began. Some took liquor home; others got drunk on the spot and, because it was extremely cold, either froze right there or fell drunk into an ice hole in the river, where self-defense finished them off. In a word, it was a scene.

Toward evening there wasn't a lot of liquor left in one of the vats. One of the looters got the idea of lighting a match to see how much was left. Of course, the fire consumed everything and everybody; there was no time to escape. A beautiful red glow stood out against the frosty, starry night, and nobody was afraid of the fire since it was far away from the houses in which people lived. At the same time, Jews were afraid of what would happen the next day, because the danger hadn't yet passed. The news about the Jewish pogrom in the shtetl circled around. Along with it circled the news that there had been many deaths in the distillery. The peasants from the villages started to ride in and look for those who hadn't returned. According to rumors, about 150 people died.

The infuriated pogromists didn't want to calm down, in addition to which a lot of peasants from neighboring villages had driven in to do some Jewish looting of their own. But the self-defense force had positioned itself along all approaches to the shtetl and didn't let them come near. They were still afraid

---

44 Prince Obolenskii's Khotimsk distillery was built in 1890.
45 Compare this incident with the memoirs of Klavdiia Borisovna Starkova, which discuss how her grandfather, the divisional doctor Mikhail Ivanovich Kotliarov, staved off an anti-Jewish pogrom in Belostok in a similar fashion. See K. B. Starkova, *Vospominaniia o perezhitom: Zhizn' i rabota semitologa-gebraista v SSSR* [Memories of the past: The life and work of a scholar of Semitic languages/Hebrew in the USSR] (St. Petersburg: Evropeiskii dom, 2006), 31.

of guns. The village constable found it unbearable that the Jews had suffered so little. He ran around to all the places where the self-defense force was and yelled, "Please take it easy!" Needless to say, they understood his intentions and, as if by accident, wounded him lightly. At this point, like a madman, he screamed that he would send a telegram to Spravnik, the regional boss, to the effect that the pogrom was in its third day, forty shops were destroyed, and Jews were shooting the pogromists. He asked for reinforcements. By chance a certain Tamarkin, a rich Jew, saw the telegram before it was sent, unceremoniously grabbed the constable by the collar, and screamed, "Write what I dictate to you, or you won't come out of this alive!" The constable caved in and wrote what Tamarkin dictated to him.

At that time Cossacks and dragoons were positioned for action against the workers' movement. There were more dragoons in Klimovichi, the nearby district seat, and everybody thought that after they got the constable's telegram they would come [to Khotimsk—MB].

Now I will describe what I was doing during the pogrom. When Father saw that they had started looting the shops, and he had to go take part in the self-defense (since he had signed up and had been going to training), he broke the windows in our house and blocked the entrance with firewood. Our stepmother wasn't home, and he took my brothers and me by the hand and led us by way of kitchen gardens to a Russian stove maker we knew. This was "our" stove maker; he often did work for us. Father himself went to his organization [self-defense—MB]. When the shops were looted and the Russians started hauling Jewish things through the streets, our stove maker also wanted a little action, and we were holding him back. He started to send us home, saying that nothing was left [the pogrom was over—MB]. I, of course, understood that there was nowhere for us to go, but my little boys started sniffling. I don't know how it would have ended, but fortunately Father arrived. He had in fact come to make sure we weren't disturbing the stove maker. He didn't wait for the stove maker to repeat his words but took us back, again through the kitchen gardens. We reached a small bathhouse and went inside, where we found another Jewish family. Father asked the woman to look after us and returned to his people. We sat there until the peasants went home. When the Jews had calmed down a little, Father came for us and told us what had happened during those days. I already told this part of his story.

Then Father said, "Sadly, we paid a heavy price." He said that Shifrin had been killed, a young Jewish man of twenty-five. He was handsome and very strong. Many people were afraid of his strength. I asked Father's permission to go to the funeral, and he said yes. All the Jews came to the funeral—young and old, as they say—as did the self-defense group from a different place, Kostiukovichi. There was a red flag with the inscription "Workers of the World, Unite!" There was also a black flag with the inscription "We Vow to Avenge Your Death." Everyone present cried. As soon as they brought in the coffin, people started singing "You Fell Victim." Then they sang funeral songs in Yiddish:

> Du bist gefalen mayn getrayer.
> Es treft dir eyn kuyl mayn getrayer.
> Mir khanun aroys,
> Glaykh fun fayer, mir geylun mir kushen dayn vund.

> You have fallen, my dear.
> You took a bullet, my dear.
> We come out from the fire
> Right from the fire, we heal, we kiss your wound.[46]

At the time these songs were very popular. Since this was the first time I had encountered such a scene, I stood and trembled. But I wanted to stay to the end. Everybody went to the cemetery. After Shifrin was buried, many people made speeches. The self-defense people who had come in from outside spoke particularly well. They urged everyone to avenge this death. They urged people to unite and rebel against tsarist power, which did nothing but make pogroms against the Jews.

On that day the shtetl was full of excitement. Nobody wanted to stay home. People said that the pogrom had ended and the self-defense group was going home. Then they said that in nearby village they [the police—MB] had set an ambush to capture the self-defense force when it came through. But the group was warned in time, and they went by a different road and arrived safely. We were happy about this. They had saved our Jews from a second pogrom.

Thus, although still a child I had already been an eyewitness to two pogroms. But the pogroms that took place in our town and in Klintsy were nothing in comparison to those that went on in Bessarabia, especially

---

46 Thanks to Lyudmila Sholokhova, Roberta Newman, and Arkadi Zeltser for their help in translation.

Kishinev.[47] History knows no bloodletting of the sort that happened there. They took Jews and sliced open their bellies and stuffed feathers inside. Jews were thrown off high buildings. They stabbed children with sabers, raised them high and impaled them one after the other. It's hard to describe how much Jewish blood flowed there.

There were also Jewish pogroms in Belorussia: Orsha, Rogachev, Shklov. In Shklov they burst into a synagogue during prayer, when men were standing in *talis un tfilen*. Tfilen are put on the arm and head. The pogromists tore pieces of flesh from men's arms and heads, where the tfilen were, then slaughtered them. Then they dragged the Torah scroll from the ark, wrapped the dead men in it, and set the synagogue on fire. Young Jews from Orsha went to Rogachev, around two hundred of them, to help defend the Jews there. When they got off the train, they were surrounded by police, and all were brutally murdered.[48] That's the kind of sorrow we endured in that time.

At that time we subscribed to Jewish newspapers and magazines. Despite the tsarist censorship, the newspapers wrote about much of this. Jews from foreign countries raised the alarm, particularly in America. There was a huge wave of emigration among Russian Jews, particularly to America, both "near America" (New York) and "far America" (Canada and Argentina). Everywhere imaginable, Jews were gathering in crowds and discussing where to go and how to pay for the trip. After the pogroms, Jews who lived abroad sent a lot of money to victims. Much of this money was used to emigrate. Usually just one person went from a family. Many crooks appeared, too, who took advantage of Jewish ignorance and credulousness. They said they were representatives of some emigration agency or other and took all their money, and the would-be emigrants were left penniless in some border town. The whole world talked about that last Jewish emigration. There had never been an emigration of that size. There was even a film in which the last [unclear—MB] ship with Jewish emigrants took off for America. It was a heart-rending scene. Even now, I can

---

47 Although in October 1905 there was a pogrom in Kishinev in which 19 Jews were killed and 56 wounded, Doba-Mera is probably retelling the horrors of the famous Kishinev pogrom of April 1903 (59 killed, 586 wounded). The worst pogrom of October 1905 took place in Odessa, with around four hundred people murdered.

48 Thirty people perished in the Orsha pogrom. We have no information about whether the police in Rogachev killed two hundred members of the Orsha self-defense; it seems unlikely. Doba-Mera's accounts of events that she did not herself witness should be understood not as facts but as a description of the general mood, which she did witness and later reevaluated under the influence of her twenty-year Soviet experience.

see it before my eyes. Of course, my father wanted to go, but there was nobody to leave us with.

So this is how Jews lived in tsarist Russia. The first thing to understand is the Pale of Settlement, where Jews were permitted to live. There weren't a lot of provinces in the Pale, so they were all crowded with Jews, mostly poor ones. They tore pieces of bread from each other's mouths, because there was nowhere for them to earn money. Sholem Aleichem described this very well. He knew and understood the whole tragedy of Jewish life to the bottom of his soul. Jews were not permitted to live in villages; they were not allowed to own and farm land. When a Jew served in the army, he could only be a simple soldier with no possibility of promotion. He was despised by everyone, beaten and hounded, and he had to suffer it in silence.[49]

Although there is considerable anti-Semitism even today, you can't compare it. Now the government punishes [anti-Semites—MB], and they are afraid, but back then the government itself supported anti-Semitism. Now they say you can't call a Jewish person a *zhid*. They'll haul you to court for it, but they won't say that a Jew is a person just like anyone else. Apparently anti-Semitism won't be rooted out any time soon. In my opinion, the only way it will be rooted out is when all children are brought up in children's homes by good teachers. Then, maybe, we'll see an end to this.

Let me return to my own life. I was living at home and not working anywhere. A relative, Blanter, told me that he had a relative in Roslavl´ who was a tailor and that he had visited him, talked to him about me, and got his agreement to give me work. Without thinking too much, I went to Roslavl´ to this tailor, and he had no need of me. It's true that he had a big workshop with a lot

---

49 When her subject is the condition of Jews in Russia, Doba-Mera has considerable knowledge. When she discusses questions of general politics and history (the revolution, World War I), she repeats then-current stereotypes and mixes things up. Jews were permitted to live in fifteen Russian provinces and ten provinces within the Kingdom of Poland that were part of the Russian Empire. Outside the Pale of Jewish Settlement, settlement was permitted only to specific categories of Jews (merchants of the first guild, individuals with a higher education, and artisans with certificates, among others). The twenty-five provinces covered a large territory. The problem was that Jews were forbidden to settle in rural areas, although there were few cities and most were small. As a result, the 5.5 million Jews in the empire were concentrated in cities and towns, in which they formed a large percentage or even a majority of the population. If you also take into account the numerous prohibitions and restrictions on education, land purchase, and occupation, as well as state, church, and popular anti-Semitism, it becomes clear why Jews, in Doba-Mera's words, "were tearing bread from one another's mouths."

of girls working for him. He let me live with him while I looked for work. Every day I paced the city backward and forward, but nobody needed anyone like me.

The workers for some reason talked to me as though I were a grownup. They told me that a certain widow Gaidukova lived in their courtyard, and that in the evening there would be a workers' meeting, and that a speaker had come from Briansk to address it. To tell the truth, I had long wanted to see what a mass meeting was—one that was, as people said then, *conspiratorial*, which means secret. Barely breathing from excitement, I couldn't wait for evening. Finally the appointed hour arrived, and we set off. There were a lot of people in the house. Only a little wick was burning, so I couldn't make out anyone's face. But when we walked in, they noticed me straight off, asked whose child I was, and hoped that I wouldn't blather about what I saw. They wouldn't have objected to making me leave, but the girl who brought me pushed me farther inside and whispered, "Get up on the stove."[50] And that's what I did.

Many people spoke, all of them saying the same thing: that the tsar must be overthrown. At the time I couldn't understand this. How could such a thing happen when he had so many soldiers and all the rich people supported him? And how could such a small group of people hope to break someone so powerful? Of course, at the time I didn't understand that this was not the only group [of its type], even though in Klintsy I had seen a crowd of several thousand people shouting, "Down with the tsar!" Although I understood very little about all this, I was happy that I was allowed into such a secret place.

Soon I found out that a young Jewish man, a member of the self-defense force, was in the hospital with a leg wound. This was Khacha Pishchik from Pochep. The master apprentice girls were going to see him and asked if I wanted to go and spend some time with someone from home. I didn't have anything else to do, so I went with them.

In the hospital I saw a pale, fair-haired young man lying in bed. He was very glad to see us. He knew the others, but not me. He paid a lot of attention to me, said he was sorry that I was so young and already had to make a living on my own. He said I lived the life of a wanderer and advised me to go home immediately. So I decided that the next day I would find an excuse and go home. But when I woke up in the morning, I was seized by horror. As I slept, my traveling money had been stolen. What could I do now? I didn't even have money to buy a roll for breakfast. Then I remembered that not far away, on a

---

50 A Russian stove, widespread throughout Russia and Belorussia, was a large stove with a bench or platform. It was used for cooking and heating.

farm, lived my uncle, my mother's brother. People said he was kind. I started asking if he ever came to the city, and if so, who he stayed with. I was sent to a hostel and told that he had been there yesterday but had returned home. They started asking me how I knew him and why I needed him. My heart was heavy, and I told them everything. Then they said I could stay and work as a chambermaid; they argued that it would be good for me. And I cried because instead of helping me, a child, they were proposing that I stay as their servant.

When they understood that I wouldn't be their servant, they told me that Uncle's daughter Nekhama Kaplan was living in town and studying at the gymnasium. I decided to ask her for help, understanding that if she was studying away from home, she had to have some money. I went to the gymnasium and waited until the school day was over. What envy I felt at that moment. Could it really be said that we were children of a brother and a sister? People took care of her, she had clothes to wear, she was content, but life was not kind to me. For a long time I didn't dare approach her; I kept walking behind. I recognized her because I had stayed at their house with my little brother the summer when my older brother had scarlet fever. She walked ahead without noticing me. I waited until she had said goodbye to her classmates and timidly walked up to her. She was happy to see me, but after she heard me out, she said that she couldn't help me and that she had no money. One thing was on my mind: how to get home?

Walking along the street, I ran into our Khotimsk driver. I told him my misfortune and asked him to take me home. He agreed right away, and I got my things and went home with him, and Father was happy to see me and paid him for bringing me. For a long time afterward I remembered my trip to Roslavl' and could not forgive Blanter for deceiving me and making me lose so much health and money. At least it ended well, as it could have been worse.

When I returned home, Father sent me to apprentice with a men's tailor. As I already wrote, seamstresses wanted a lot of money, and they took on apprentices for a long time; tailors didn't take money, and the apprenticeships were for one year, after which they promised to pay a salary. Father, of course, didn't take into account that as a girl I would be surrounded by nothing but men. And workers in those days were crude. There were a lot of drunkards and scoundrels among them, while among women, in a seamstress's workshop, this wasn't the case. I didn't understand this at the time, but even if I had, I wouldn't have dared to contradict Father. I went to work before Passover, around April. My boss was called Mendel; his last name was Itskov. He wasn't a bad man. He had a big family, a wife and many children. In addition to me, there were two people working for him: a master apprentice, an assistant master, and me, a pupil. From the first days I understood that I was going to have a rough time, as I wasn't used to cursing and foul language from childhood. The boss, it's true, treated me with respect. Knowing that I was from a good family, he tried not to use foul language in front of me. My boss lived very poorly. He himself did not sew a lot because he spent entire days running around looking for business. He worked at night, at which time he also prepared work for us to do during the day.

Despite my hateful new life, I quickly accepted my fate. I worked for my boss but ate and slept at home. I learned quickly, and the boss and the workers could not stop praising me and my talent. But at home, my position worsened. My stepmother did not hesitate to tell me not to eat at home. My out-of-season work ran from seven in the morning until seven in the evening. In the middle I had an hour for dinner. And when there was more work, nobody looked at the clock. When I returned home tired, she would begrudge me food, and that was harder for me than working. With every day it became clearer to me that in the home where I had been born and had by now almost grown up, I was a stranger. Nonetheless, no matter how tired I was, when I got home from work, I did all the housework. On Thursdays after work I spent all night tidying and cleaning for the Sabbath, and in the morning, without sleep, I would go to work.

It's understandable that life was difficult for me. I worked without pay; I had nothing to wear; I went around in rags. I was often allowed to bring finished work to customers. The boss tried to send me. Customers would give tips, and the tips were divided among the workers. If the other workers were sent, they took the tip for themselves and would say that there hadn't been one. I was honest, and as a result some pennies came my way. Because of these pennies, I was able at least to wash myself in the bathhouse and buy something cheap.

It was the summer of 1906. A young man came to work for us from the district seat, Klimovichi. He was thin, dark, and quite ugly. He had a porcelain flute, on which he played after work. Right away, I saw that he was different from the other workers. He spoke good Russian, and he didn't curse or use foul language. He had a lot of books, and he read a lot. I started to see that he didn't look like a tailor. I seized a moment when we wouldn't be heard and asked him if he had been working for a long time. He answered that it had been only three years. He said that he had been an extern, but as he had had nothing to live on, he became a tailor. Indeed, he looked more like a nonmatriculated student than a tailor. His first name was Liova, but he didn't tell me his last name. Why would someone from a big city come to our backwater and not say his last name?

When he had worked with us for a while, Liova asked if we could read. When he found out that we could, he started to offer us books. I seized them gladly. There were books in Yiddish and in Russian. Liova often asked us to talk about what we had read. Then he began to give out pamphlets in Yiddish and Russian. The Russian pamphlets were put out by the Moscow publishing house Donskaia rech'. As I later learned, these pamphlets were very popular among ordinary people. They talked about the hardship of life among the people and about the heartless rich. The Yiddish books were in the same spirit, only I don't remember the titles. I liked these little books a great deal, and I gladly read as many as I had time for.

I had the same girlfriends, but their lives were easier; they didn't work anywhere but only helped their mothers at home. When I had free time, I went for walks with them, but even at our age we had different views. Only one girl, Rakhil'—her father was a tanner and she worked for him—was almost like me. We were different only because at home she was a needed member of the family, and I was not. They lived very poorly. Young working people used to gather at their house and read books and newspapers and talk about the social structure of the country. Such was my childhood at this time.

One summer day after work I went with my girlfriends to walk along Barabanovka Street. The street was on the other side of the river, where everybody used to go walking. Jews were allowed to walk but not to live there. A landowner lived there by the name of Robert. He couldn't stand Jews, but as our shtetl was in Mogilev Province, and Jews were permitted to live there, he got the government to make his street part of Orel Province, where Jews were forbidden to live. And he got all the Jews sent away from there. The empty houses where the Jews had lived were boarded up, and nobody would buy them because the Russians were confident that they would get everything anyway.

So on the Sabbath and holidays everybody would stroll there. The street was beautiful, with a lot of greenery, and so everybody liked to stroll along it. One time, when I was walking with my girlfriends, a sturdy young man named Shifrin began to walk behind us. People said he was a *democrat*. These were people who were against the tsar. At first we didn't pay any attention to him, but then we became convinced that he was following us. Being very young, we got embarrassed and started off for home. Apparently he heard our conversation and turned to me. "Miss," he said, "please, excuse yourself to your girlfriends. I have to have a word with you about something important." He said that the new master apprentice Liova had told him about me, had said that I understood things and was different from the other girls in our shtetl and that even grownups could not grasp things that I could. He explained to me simply and in detail why I lived poorly, and why the Rivkin girls from the same town lived well. He explained to me that for everyone to live the same, workers must unite and overthrow the tsar, and then life would be better. He told me that even our shtetl had a big organization and that it had to be kept secret. He asked me if I would like to join their organization. I asked if there was anyone as young as me. "Of course not," he answered. "But I will vouch for you, because you are a very intelligent girl. Only, it's a *conspiracy*." That meant that not a soul should know what he had said to me.

My girlfriends were waiting for me at home. They pressed me with questions about what he had been saying to me for so long. I said that first we talked about work and then about books. My answer did not satisfy them. I became a puzzle for them, and they kept looking suspiciously at me. And I felt that from that day forward I became different, not the same as before. For if I had been chosen, and not my girlfriends, to receive this secret, then probably I was different from them in some way. When I came to work, the master apprentices greeted me with a smile. Apparently they knew what had happened. But I pretended not to notice.

Now I understood why Liova, our master apprentice, came from the city to work with us. And how come he hadn't told us his last name? That means he was being followed by the police. As before, I read the books he gave me and understood what they were saying. The master apprentices started talking freely in front of me, which they hadn't done before, and I had often felt uncomfortable at the thought that I was in their way. But now I was very happy that when the boss was gone we would discuss various questions.

Liova told me that he had a book by Karl Marx called *Political Economy*,[51] and that Marx was a wise man who wrote about the hardships of working people's lives. He said it would be hard for me to read a book like that on my own, so in his free time he would study it with me. And that's what we did. I liked this book a lot and listened to his explanations with great interest.

One day our workers announced that there would be a mass meeting, meaning an underground one. I had attended such a meeting once before, in Roslavl′, but there I didn't know anyone, and here everyone was a friend. The meeting was held in a forest that belonged to the landowner Robert, the one who kicked the Jews off his street. If he only knew what was going on in his forest, he would have made all Russia stand on end. It turned out that

---

51 There is no such book written by Karl Marx. Presumably Doba-Mera means his *Capital*.

I did know a lot of people, but all of them were grownups. When they saw me, some of them asked each other who brought me here and could I keep a secret? Suddenly there was a cry, "He's coming! He's coming!" The invited speaker had arrived, and the meeting began. A patrol was stationed in a circle around the group and let in only those who knew the password (a word agreed on in advance). At the meeting were many people, including Asia, the sister of my girlfriend Rakhil′. Sometime later, I asked Asia to bring Rakhil′ into the organization too, since she was very intelligent and read a lot, and then I would not be alone. Now I was really happy. Rakhil′ and I did all the tasks that were assigned to us. They sent us places where grownups couldn't show themselves, while we attracted no attention at all. We did guard duty together, directing comrades to the meeting while we ourselves picked wildflowers without arousing the suspicion of anybody passing by. In the basement of Rakhil′'s house was an underground printing press. It was run by her sister's fiancé, Aizik Riabinkii. He was beloved by the masses. He didn't have an orator's skills, but he chaired meetings and led the organization very well.

We had one other girlfriend who by the standards of the time was educated and well-read and considered an intellectual. Her father owned a pharmacy, but they lived very poorly. Her name was also Rakhil′; her last name was Berlin. When the two of us separated from the group, she understood what was going on and started asking us not to leave her alone, so we had to ask the leaders to confirm to us that she could be considered trustworthy.

We three girls did so much work for the organization that nobody would believe it. The entire group was divided into sections, since it would have meant the end of the group if it met together in its entirety very often. Rakhil′ Berlina and I were asked to lead groups; I was given a group of fifteen people, and so was she. Our work meant getting them together and reading books to them, as the majority at that time could not read. We discussed various questions, and despite our youth the groups respected us.

In that way time passed. Workers started to complain that they did not have enough money to live on and that they worked many hours. A strike was organized. In response, some owners promised a lockout, and others threatened to call in the police. It ended well, in a victory for the workers. I played an active role in that strike, checking the workshops myself. Workers of various types joined the tailors.

People started coming to see me at home, and my stepmother started pestering Father to make me leave, since I was underage and he was legally responsible for anything I did. Autumn arrived; it was already impossible to have either mass meetings or small groups in the forest. People started to visit me. Father liked the fact that people were reading and discussing questions, but he was very afraid for himself and for me. Every time after they left, he would ask me how this would end. If I were arrested, than nobody would be able to intercede for me, and he, as the father, would suffer. Occasionally there would be a mass meeting in the winter, somewhere in a field, in an old bathhouse. At night people walked through waist-high snow. It was very difficult. Riabinkii got in touch with the organization in Gomel′, and they started sending literature and other necessary things. The organization grew.

In the spring of 1907, my stepmother insisted that I leave home before I ruined the family. I had to change jobs because my former boss couldn't give me meals. Now I was getting room and board and a salary—just pennies. But I was satisfied with this, because I was making my own living. At the same time, I kept working in the organization, gaining the respect of all the comrades. What the organization was called did not interest me. I knew only that they wanted to overthrow the tsar, and when that happened, everything would be good. I understood that more people meant greater power, but how to make this happen was impossible for me to figure out.

One evening, when Rakhil′ Berlina and I were out walking, a comrade came over to us and told us not to go home, because we were needed. Late in the evening a driver picked us up. The night was moonless. As we were leaving the shtetl, the driver said that the owner of the horses was also a comrade, and that we were carrying leaflets to the village of Besovitskaia, not far from there, and that the leaflets would have to be handed over.[52] We drove up to a house where, it seemed, Pimen-Brui was living. We gave him one package, and the others we tossed along the road at various places as we drove home. By the time we returned, it was already getting light. The work had been successful. In the morning the people of Khotimsk were saying that there were democrats in the village, that leaflets were appearing on the streets.

When summer came, we again began meeting outside. We chose a place in a wooded area. So as not to arouse the suspicions of people who lived nearby, some of us arrived by circuitous paths, while others came in rowboats. A representative from Gomel′ also came. The meeting lasted until late in the evening. Suddenly the patrol raised an alarm. The crowd got frightened and wanted to disperse, but Riabinkii yelled in a voice he didn't usually use,

---

52 The text has Bisovitski, which may be the Polish name. Thanks to Leonid Smilovitskii for pointing out the village's present-day name.

"Comrades! Nobody move! The first thing we have to do is assure the safety of our comrade from Gomel′. Close ranks immediately. Whoever has a weapon, get it ready." That's how I found out that we had weapons. We immediately closed ranks behind our strongest boys, among whom was Yoshe-Iche (Iosif Slutsker). Everybody rose and took their places. The invited comrade was put into the first rowboat along with someone else, and then gradually the remaining comrades were sent off. The boats were overcrowded, very low in the water. Barely alive, we got ourselves home; someone lost a shoe, someone lost something else, but nobody found anything. It was morning when we reached home. It turned out that the alarm was caused by some guards investigating where people were going. But they had been afraid to come close, since there were a lot of us and very few of them. After the adventures of that night it took us a long time to get back to normal.

But I haven't described how we celebrated May 1. The night before we had a mass meeting. A speaker talked about the meaning of May 1 and told us how to mark the occasion. It was decided not to go to work on that day but to appear at a specific time at a specific place. Rowboats were waiting for us there. First the boats traveled one by one, and then, when they had arrived at a deserted spot, all of them came together. A red flag made an appearance. There was a meeting, and then we sang the International. Then we sat down on the beautiful empty shore, read newspapers and pamphlets, and sang many songs that were at that time forbidden. Toward evening we returned home. I will never forget this day. When we returned to work, our bosses were furious. "You'll pay for this," they said. "The chief of police will be on your case."

Indeed, soon after this, our underground work was cut off. Here's how it happened.

A Zionist circle formed among us. They called themselves the S-S.[53] Their goal was to organize the emigration of Jews to Palestine, as in their opinion Palestine should belong to the Jews, although there were Turks and Arabs there. The idea was for rich people to go there and buy land from the Turks, and then for all Jews to gather there. We all made fun of them [the Zionists—MB], even composing several sarcastic songs about them. But one day, on a Saturday in 1907, a Zionist representative came, someone they were in contact with.

---

53 S-S is an abbreviation for Zionist-Socialists (Territorialists). The Zionist-Socialist Workers' Party was founded in 1904, with a platform of unifying Jews in their own territory, not necessarily Erets Yisroel (Palestine), so that the Jewish proletariat could carry out the class struggle for socialism there. In May 1917 the S-S merged with the ESRP (the Jewish Socialist Workers' Party) into a single United Jewish Socialist Workers' Party (*fareynikte* in Yiddish).

And together with other organizations, they set up a mass meeting to debate which party was better.

We met in a wooded area belonging to a landowner. Their speaker said that there was a lot of anti-Semitism in Russia, and that it would never come to an end, and that the only solution for the Jews was to go to Palestine. Our people objected that it wasn't true, that things were bad because of the autocracy, and when the autocracy was overthrown, then we would have equality and brotherhood. We all needed to struggle together against the tsar; then we would be more powerful. Our struggle was not about nationality but about class. If the Jews went to Palestine, they would break their backs for Jewish capitalists, and in the end it makes no difference who is exploiting you, a rich Jew or a rich Russian. We should now and forever cast off the yoke of capital, and then Russia would be our motherland.

Everyone argued and yelled for a long time, forgetting the need for caution. They got so carried away, they thought the revolution had come. Suddenly, when the debates were in full swing, there was a scream: "Police! We've been surrounded!" And it was true. The first thing we did was help the leader take cover. Whoever had weapons or illegal literature threw it into the bushes. When we were completely surrounded, the police gave a shout, "Hands up!" Frightened, we all complied. There was a command: "March!" They escorted us out of the woods and marched us along the streets to the police station. Only when we got to the street did I see how many of our people had been arrested. The news quickly spread throughout the shtetl. People whose children had not come home ran to find out if they were among those arrested. We marched along, all together, as thought we were at a demonstration. Police surrounded us. People from the shtetl came running from all sides. Those who got too close to the police were struck with rifle butts. That's what happened to a woman named Golubeva. Something happened to her lungs, and she died. By the time they had marched us to the house where the police chief lived, the crowd was so huge that people who were under arrest started mingling with free people. The police went crazy, using their nightsticks and rifle butts, but still some people managed to disappear into the crowd and run off. I was among them. I was smaller than anyone, and the police didn't pay a lot of attention to me. When we were marched off, I was in the middle, and when we arrived, I made my way to the edge of the group. A woman from the crowd shielded me with her body, and I took off as fast as my legs could carry me and found shelter with people I knew.

Everybody they detained was arrested, but the next day they were let free after they signed a paper agreeing that they would no longer meet. In addition, the police chief was bribed into letting them go. Nobody dared hold a meeting again because we were followed at every step.

Naturally everybody mocked us. If earlier, nobody knew who belonged to the organization, after the arrest everybody found out. People would ask, "So, crybabies, have you overthrown Nicholas? You got off easy. They should have been tougher."

At that time I was working for my second boss and living with his family. They lived next door to my father. My little brothers often ran to see me, but I only went home on the Sabbath to change my clothes. I worked a lot, even at night. My boss was young but sly as a fox, and he had a voracious appetite for money. My previous boss had been poor, but he was a good man and had a lot of compassion for me. This one was the opposite, a typical exploiter. But I had no other option, and I gave in to the inevitable. One day I decided to leave him, and here is why.

I was sitting at his family's table and having dinner. At that time some customers arrived, including Gitta Rivkina, the daughter of a rich neighbor, a grown young woman. Seeing that I was eating, she asked in surprise, "Are you actually boarding here? How could that be? A father's only daughter, and the father lives next door, and the daughter doesn't live with him." These words consumed me like fire; tears came to my eyes, and leaving my dinner, I sat down to work. That is when I got the idea of leaving Khotimsk. May I forget the pain of being a stranger in my own home, and may people not condemn my father.

I told my boss that I was leaving, but he didn't want to let me go, since I brought him a good income. He refused to pay me what I was due on a variety of pretexts. With difficulty, I pried some money from him and told my father that I was leaving, explaining the reason. He sighed but said nothing. He did not ask me not to go but to live at home, because he was afraid of his wife.

Now came the question of where to go. My "kind" uncle Alter had a brother who was a tailor in Pochep, so that's where I was sent. A wagon turned up right away, and I left. The ride with horses took two days and two nights.

I arrived. He was a boss like any other. We agreed on three rubles a month, plus room and board. Also, before I left I got a contact address and password from my old (Khotimsk) underground committee, which meant that if there was an underground organization in my new place, I could join it and I wouldn't be alone.

My work began in Pochep. My boss liked my work. He lived well. After work they made me scrub the floors and do other menial jobs. Once, tired after work, I hit my head against a broken lampshade and shattered it. They made me pay for it out of my first wages, as though it were new. I made friends with some girls, among whom was the daughter of a poor watchmaker, Belodubrovskii. She was fifteen years old. She was healthy and full of energy; only she wore glasses. When I had got to know her a little better, I found out that they had an underground apartment. "Politicals" who were hiding from the police would find shelter there and monetary help. For a long time she was afraid to let me visit her, but when I showed her the password, she stopped being afraid and said that there was no organization, that everyone had been arrested and sent into exile. There was only some money left in the support fund.

Through her I became acquainted with some comrades, both Russians and Jews. All of them showed a fatherly concern for my life. When they found out how difficult things were for me, they set me up with a new boss. When I moved, once again, I was not paid.

The boss at my new place was very rich. He had a big tailoring workshop and many old tailors working for him. His wife had a big flour business. This was his second wife, and she had many children of her own. From his first wife he had only an unlucky little girl who was missing an arm. Despite her father's wealth, the crippled little girl did all sorts of difficult jobs, and when her stepmother came home, she used to beat her mercilessly for no reason. I couldn't bear this. When she beat her, I cried, and as a result the wife took a dislike to me.

I walked around barefoot and in rags. Once a customer came in, a young man. Looking at my face and dress, he asked the workers, when I had turned away in embarrassment at how I looked, "This girl has a very intelligent face. Why is she dressed in such rags?" Then he inquired about who I was and where I was from. It turned out that he had been friends with my mother. He was very distressed to learn that my mother had died young, and I was living under such conditions.

In the meantime, the crippled little girl was getting attacked more and more often. Once when we were working and the girl was holding the baby, sitting by a vacant machine, the stepmother came out of nowhere and hit her head so hard that the little girl's forehead hit the machine and blood started to flow. When she screamed and I saw her bloody forehead, I couldn't calm down and decided to leave.

I didn't tell my comrades that I had left my new boss; I was afraid they would again start worrying about me. I went to a shop, where there was a tailor who had just then arrived from Starodub, to ask for work. He said that he wanted to open a workshop in the village of Zheriatin, not far, about thirty-five kilometers from Pochep. He was in town to find workers. He proposed good conditions and said he would pay for the trip. To be honest, I didn't like the new boss, but I had no other option and I went with him to the village. We traveled with horses, as the railroad didn't go there. It was September; the days were sunny, but the nights were cold.

Let me describe my new boss's life and circumstances. He was tall and young, a handsome man concerned about his own appearance. He talked a lot and lied even more. His wife was a dirty, greasy, nasty woman. They had a lot of children, all small. Poverty lurked in every corner of their apartment. The children were hungry and in rags, and nobody looked after them. No sooner had I crossed the threshold than horror seized me. "My God! Where have I ended up, and how can I get out of here?"[54]

The first thing that struck me was how the landlady kneaded bread. Her hands were dirty; her hair was uncombed and uncovered. She would knead, then wipe her nose with her hand, and then stick her hand into the dough. Her children stood around her and yelled, "Knead faster! We want to eat."

I was terrified. I would have to live like that too! Having traveled such a long distance, I was hungry. I took out what I had left from the road and sat down to eat. The boss's children watched me enviously. I gave them everything I had and on the orders of the boss sat down to work, but my work didn't go well. The boss approved, saying that it was always that way at a new place.

From the boss's children I learned that the settlement was a wealthy one, that it was in Orel Province, where Jews were forbidden to live. In the village was one other Jewish tailor, a rich man; he bribed the police to let him live there. My own boss had passed his artisan's test, which gave him the right to live outside the Pale.

Then I asked how I could stay there. I didn't have the right to live outside the Pale. To that, the children responded that their father had talked to the police sergeant, and added, "If you're bad, the constable will march you home

---

54 One gets the sense that Doba-Mera is not seeking work or trying to take part in the revolutionary movement so much as looking for a way to overcome her loneliness, to find a home or a group of people who could replace her family and family circle. This is, naturally, the one thing she cannot find, and so she often moves from place to place.

with prisoners, whenever Father tells him to." I understood that my position was even worse than I thought.

The Sabbath came. News that my boss had brought me reached the workers for the other tailor. It turned out that there were a few families of Jewish artisans who lived in the village. When, on that Sabbath, I went out into the street after dinner, Jewish girls and boys my age suddenly surrounded me, as though they had emerged from underground. It turned out that somebody from home, my girlfriend's brother, worked here. This boy was older than me, and he was startled to find me here. He introduced me to everybody, and we went through the fields to visit with young people in the neighboring village. It was great fun. We sang songs and played. As the day came to an end, I didn't want to return to my boss. My new acquaintances advised me not to stay with him. But where could I go, and to whom? Who needed me? I was a stranger to the whole world.

My new acquaintances got permission from their boss for me to stay until I found a driver who would take me to the city for free. But who did I have in the city? Did anyone want to see me? Disgusted with the whole world and cursing the day I was born, I got my things from the boss and started to live with people I barely knew. The workers were very supportive, however, and that raised my spirits.

Around that time, my boss's chronically ill, paralyzed grandson died. He had to be buried in the city, as the village didn't have a Jewish cemetery. So it was necessary to take the dead child to Pochep. Observant Jews have a law that a Jewish body cannot be accompanied by a non-Jew, and that it must always be in the presence of at least one Jewish soul. They hired a wagon to transport the body, but nobody wanted to travel with it. The lot fell to me. Of course, nobody asked my opinion, and I had to go anyway, because I didn't have the means to remain in the village nor anyone to stay with. They sat me next to the dead body and the peasant driver, and we set off. We had traveled only a short distance when night fell, cold and dark. We drove, as I remember, through the forest. I sat and was afraid to move; I closed my eyes and was afraid to open them and see the body. The whole time I kept imagining that he was chasing us. I had never seen him alive, and now he seemed frightening to me. That's the kind of sweet life I was living, and that's why my health was ruined.

Finally we reached Pochep. It was one o'clock in the morning. As we drove through the city, I saw my comrades Mania Belodubrovskaia and Meilakh Tsipin. I shouted to them and told them about my adventures. They invited me to come with them, but I told them I was with a body and that I had to turn it over to the funeral society. Tsipin got very upset and took my place. He freed me and sent me to sleep at Mania's, ordering me firmly, like a father, "Don't go anywhere until I come for you."

When I got to Mania's, I started envying her a little. She had a place to call home. She wasn't a stranger to anyone. She didn't have a mother, but her father, even though he was poor, had not remarried, and she did not have a stepmother. Why was I so unhappy in all ways? If it hadn't been for Mania, where would I have spent the night? My father couldn't look after me; my mother would not rise from the grave. So, crying bitter tears, I fell asleep toward morning.

By the time I woke up, Mania was already at work, and Tsipin was sitting and talking with Mania's father. Mania's father was a kind, caring old man; he didn't let me go without breakfast. Then Tsipin and I left. When we got out onto the street, he said, "Come to my boss. I'll work things out with him, you'll work with me, and I won't let you come to harm." So I started working for a new boss. He was like all bosses, but quiet by nature. His wife was a pretty, stupid young woman and a real lazybones. She was sloppy and couldn't keep house. They had two children, a little boy and a little girl, very cute. I liked it better there than any place I had ever been before. All the workers were men; they treated me with respect.

When I had worked for a while, the boss's wife tried to make me scrub the floors, but the workers protested to the boss, and I got out of it. Like everybody at that time, I worked a lot and earned very little. Autumn came, and I had no winter clothes. I didn't even have an old coat. Since the time when my things were taken in the pogrom, including my coat, nobody would buy me another one, so all I had was my dress. At least I was living in the same place where I worked, so I didn't catch cold. But there was no way that I could even think about taking a walk on the Sabbath. Then my comrades at work decided together that whoever was first to get paid would buy me something to wear. I didn't know about this agreement, until suddenly my old friend Tsipin asked me to go with him to buy an inexpensive coat for myself. The offer scared me a little. Living always in such harsh conditions, I didn't trust anybody, and I had heard my share of stories about certain men who would try to win over girls, especially girls who were alone. So, first, I got upset over this offer. And second, I was afraid that because of it I would have to find a new place to work. But it turned out that this Tsipin was a very honorable man; all he wanted was for me not to get sick. Then the workers asked the boss to persuade me to accept a loan on the condition that he would withhold money every month from my wages. I believed the boss, and we all went together and bought me a pretty black jacket and galoshes. I still felt bad until I had repaid the debt. When that was out of the way, I thanked everyone and was very happy that I had bought myself clothes out of my own earnings.

Winter was coming to an end. The boss had a sister, a bride ready for the taking, all the money she needed. Suitors came to visit but weren't interested. Strangely, when they became acquainted with me, they asked the workers to tell me that they liked me. I was worried that I would lose my job over this. Even the boss's wife once said to me that I was lucky because everybody liked me. I understood that this didn't bring her any joy—on the contrary. Then I decided to leave the house when the suitors were visiting. If this was after work, then I went across the entryway to the landlady's and spent the evening there.

But one day a father and son came from Briansk to find a wife for the son. They were relatives of the family, and so they came to stay with him. They came during working hours. I was poorly dressed and the only girl among men, and I was shy in front of outsiders. The guests were rich. The suitor-to-be was well-built and handsome, well-dressed, twenty-five to twenty-eight years old. There was no question of my leaving work, because we had a rush order. Turning toward the window and lowering my head, I continued working. My comrades, understanding the reason, made fun of me, which hurt me even more.

The guests freshened up after their travels and went about their business, and I breathed freely. In the evening after work I went for a walk. When I got back, I found the table set with good things to eat, and at the table sat the visitors and some local guests. My arrival created some kind of disturbance. I was embarrassed, and saying that I had to go, I went to the landlady's and didn't return until everyone had gone their separate ways. In the morning the boss's wife said with a spiteful smile that I had made a good impression on the visitors, both father and son. I wanted to snap back a crude, sharp retort, but out of respect for my subordinate position I swallowed the offense and forced myself to say nothing. This situation caused me a lot of anxiety. I was perfectly aware of my position, and conversations like that tore my heart into pieces. Because I had already grown up, people regarded me as a potential match, and I didn't have anyone to share my feelings with. At that time I couldn't imagine greater happiness than to exchange two words with my own mother. I knew I was still very young, but looking in the mirror I saw that I was genuinely grown up, I looked older than I was, and people had reason not to believe I was still very young.

When the time came for dinner, I went to wash my hands. At that point the father of the potential groom approached me and started talking about different things, in part about who I was and where I was from. It turned out that he knew my whole family. Then he started trying to persuade me to marry his son. He praised his son and his son's wealth and said that he was ready to visit my father and ask his consent. I was embarrassed and turned him down, saying I was too young and there was still time for me to marry. As he left he asked my boss and his wife to persuade me, but in vain.

Spring came. There was a lot of work. Between Purim and Passover is only a month, and during that month I barely slept, I was working so hard. True, the boss promised a present for the work that was done. Before Passover I looked like a shadow, I got sick, my head was spinning, I had pains in my chest. Then spring passed, and the out-of-season period began. There was little work; the workers left for various places. My old comrade Tsipin was among them. I got sick, and at my boss's urging I went to see a doctor. The doctor examined me and said I was overwrought and needed rest. I sent a letter home. My father was worried but wrote that it was not a good idea to come home, because with my stepmother around I would have no rest. In conclusion he said that if rest was what I needed, I should go to my aunt in Klintsy. Although from the moment of my mother's death I knew that I didn't have a home, his words confirmed this yet again.

At that time I got a letter and a little package from Aunt Gesia in Klintsy. In the package was a silk elastic belt of a kind very fashionable at the time, and a white summer parasol. Although Auntie didn't invite me to visit, nevertheless I decided to go. I did it because I had no other options and because I knew what my fate was—always to turn up where nobody needed me. So I got my wages from my boss, promised to return for the new season, and went to my aunt in Klintsy.

1908. Aunt Gesia was very welcoming. Everybody liked how I had become a person, as they put it. I told them I had been ill and needed rest. The weather was good in Klintsy. A traveling circus owned by someone named Andrzhevskii had set up a tent. To interest the public, after showing some circus routines they gave away big prizes. This attracted many people, and there was a big crowd.

Uncle had a little boy, around twelve years old, by the name of Davidka, who later died. Auntie told him to take me and show me the circus. We went together to buy tickets. Even though I was only sixteen, I looked older. When we got to the circus, as usually happens in the provinces when people see someone new, everyone wanted to know who I was. People started coming over to my little nephew and asking who I was. Freida Medvedeva was one of them. When she found out that I was a relative, she started a conversation with me, asking where I lived and if I was going to stay here long. She didn't stop praising me, which I really disliked. She said that Auntie would probably not let me go anywhere else. As we were talking, a small, black-headed fellow took her aside and asked, as I heard, who I was. I didn't have time to answer when he bounded over to my side and said, "Allow me to make your acquaintance. I am your relative, Medvedev." I was so startled by this unexpected and, by my standards at the time, audacious act that I didn't know what to say. Recovering a little, I took my leave and my nephew and went home.

Back at the house Auntie asked if we had bought tickets, but looking at me, she understood that something had happened. My little nephew explained everything, and she had such a laugh that I got even more offended and started crying. She, of course, hurried to comfort me and explained that I was no longer a child, that it was good that people were taking an interest in me, and that the young man behaved very well. But I was unconvinced and insisted that if he was well-behaved, he wouldn't have done that. Then Auntie said, "Don't spit in the puddle; you'll have to drink from it." This meant that I shouldn't make fun of people and that strangers can become intimates. To which I answered that I was in no danger of drinking, and the conversation ended. But I didn't go to the circus because I was afraid of meeting my new acquaintances.

I rested a little and put on some weight. But having become accustomed to work, I was bored without it. Auntie told me I shouldn't go away any more but should find work in Klintsy. She didn't like the fact that I was working for a men's tailor and tried to find me a place with a seamstress. But since I was inexperienced in this work, seamstresses didn't want to pay me, and I decided to seek work in my own specialty. One day on the street I met an old comrade from the organization, with whom I had worked for a time in Khotimsk. He was sincerely happy to see me and advised me to work in their workshop—that is, for his boss—since the new season was starting.

My new boss's name was Perlin. He was an old Jew with a beard down to his waist. I earned thirteen rubles a month, without board. I would have to live at Auntie's and eat there. The boss was rich. He had around fifteen people working for him, many of them with families, including his relatives. I was the only woman. The workers were relatively well-mannered and behaved respectfully to me, as was always the case. The boss, it is true, also tried to please me, but that was because I was related to Belkin, his rich customer. At that time I had a lot of relatives in Klintsy. These were my mother's brothers and their children. Before I started working, they ran after me and were interested in me, but when they found out that I was working for a tailor and, even worse, among men, they were afraid they would lose their status because of me. I understood this and myself started to avoid meetings with them. Gradually I made the acquaintance of girls at my level, and I wasn't bored with them. I worked a lot, and on work days I didn't feel like going out because I came home tired. I spent Sabbaths with my friends. My girl cousins made a lot of themselves and so were always alone. When they would meet me in a happy group, they would ask me to introduce them to my girlfriends. To which I always answered, "Why should you risk your status? You're daughters of the boss and we are artisans. Nothing will make us understand each other." They lived on their parents' money, and we lived on what we earned with our hands.

Autumn was coming, and with it the Jewish holidays. The workers said that it was easier to pull the boss's teeth than to extract money from him. He didn't like paying, though at first he paid me well. When I got my first wages from him, I sent Father ten rubles for the holiday. I was so happy that I was able to help Father. I sent him some money on a few occasions in the winter also.

At that time, a young man from Rogachev started working with us. His name was David; his last name was Goz. He had already been through the draft; he was a skilled artisan; he made good wages. Such a handsome man I had never seen. But since I had not been accustomed to paying attention to anybody, I didn't pay attention to him either. He was given a workplace next to mine. The boss's daughter went crazy over him, and I was asked to advise him to make a match with her. The boss himself asked me to do this. I felt very awkward. That kind of assignment was not to my taste and wasn't suitable for someone my age. After he had worked for a while, he asked me to introduce him to my friends. I saw that he was of good character, well-read, and terribly handsome; my girlfriends would like him. I agreed to his request, and my girlfriends were happy.

As I had promised the boss to raise the matter of his daughter, they often asked me about this. When I finally broached the subject with him, he got offended and said that he did not sell his feelings for money, and that he would be happy to take a girl without money, someone like me. I pretended that I didn't understand his hint, and when the boss asked me the next time, I told him about the refusal. Naturally, the boss's relationship to him immediately deteriorated, but he endured it and continued working. Though I didn't understand a lot at the time, I saw that he treated me with a great deal of respect but was afraid to speak up, fearing a refusal. He asked an older woman he knew to speak with Aunt Gesia. When I returned from work one evening, Auntie told me about it, asked me many questions about him, and in general wanted to know if I liked him. I was very disturbed that at my age they were already planning to marry me off, so I answered that as a friend and comrade he was very fine, but that I wasn't thinking of anything else. Having received that answer, he decided to leave.

At that time my father came to try to find work in Klintsy. Auntie didn't like that; she didn't want her poor brother to compromise her position. And there would be additional problems and expenses. In short, she forbade him to do it. He understood perfectly well, but since he didn't want to return to Khotimsk because of his material circumstances, he decided to go back to Ekaterinoslavl´, where he had once lived. This was a big city, where Jews could live and even suffer from hunger, because there were so many of them. Of course, there were rich Jews among them, but 90 percent were paupers who hung around every day looking for some way to earn a crust of bread. At night they slept on the street, because they had no money to pay for lodging. That was the fate that awaited my father too. When he was leaving, David and I accompanied him to the station. I introduced them. My father had heard about him from Auntie and seized the moment to have a conversation with him. He asked David for his father's address in Ekaterinoslavl´, then said to me quietly, "If his father is rich, I'll let you marry him, but if he's poor I won't." That's how people looked at a match in those days. If the groom was rich, then he didn't need my consent. Of course, my father can't be blamed for this. It's simply that, having lived his whole life in poverty, he wanted his children to be free from want. After my father's departure, because of the spoiled relations with his boss, David asked for his wages and soon left for his father's in Ekaterinoslavl´. He soon sent a letter in which he wrote that he had set himself up well and found a good place for me. Of course, I wasn't planning on going anywhere, since I couldn't forget my life in Pochep. All the more so as life at Auntie's wasn't at all bad. If there were slights, I tried not to notice them, because they were under no obligation to help me, so thanks to them for what they did. The other uncles and aunts didn't let me past the threshold, and here they gave me a corner, and they fed me, and I was very grateful for that and had no intention of going anywhere. From my father I received sad letters that he hadn't yet earned anything and kept hoping that he would get lucky. He also wrote that David's parents lived in a cellar and were very poor and that he wouldn't let me marry someone like that.

But David continued to write. His letters were pleasant to read: his good handwriting and intelligence added to their interest. It was pleasant to get letters like that. They were the letters of a friend.

Spring arrived. Father, who had suffered through Ekaterinoslavl´ without finding his luck, returned to Khotimsk, but his hard life in the city left its mark.

He had often been eating nothing but bread, and when he got home, he developed a stomach illness.

1909. Around May I returned home to find my father ill, and I learned that he had a serious disease of the stomach (cancer) and that the Khotimsk doctors were advising him to go to Kiev for an operation. I, of course, was quite frightened by this unwanted turn of events, especially after Auntie told me to accompany him. He was examined by doctors in Klintsy, but they too had nothing to offer. There was no way out: we had to go to Kiev. But where could we find money for the trip? I asked my boss for my wages. He got angry and seriously underpaid me, but I was happy to have what he did give. Auntie also contributed some money. Before handing it over, in the manner of rich people she gave me a lecture about how to handle money, even your own money, about how to value every cent because it was earned with great effort, and that even greater care must be taken with other people's money.

Being around sixteen years old, I had never before been in a big city. During my first encounter with a big city I would be poorly dressed, with little money, and in the company of a sick father. The very thought terrified me. Before our departure Auntie gave me an address to go to, as at that time it was not easy for a Jew to enter Kiev. Kiev itself was outside the Pale of Settlement, and Jews were not permitted to live there.[55] But there were people there who did have legal residency; these were Jewish recruits from the time of Nicholas I—they were called cantonists—and one could go to them.[56] Since they paid off the police, it was possible to stay with them for a short time. Auntie also gave us a

---

55 In January 1909 there were up to 50,000 officially registered Jews out of a general population of 470,000 ("Kiev," in *Evreiskaia entsiklopediia* (Jewish encyclopedia) [St. Petersburg: Brokhaus and Efron, c. 1910] 9:526). For more on Jewish Kiev, see Natan M. Meir, *Kiev, Jewish Metropolis: A History, 1859–1914* (Bloomington: Indiana University Press, 2010).

56 The reference is to sons of Russian private soldiers who from 1805 to 1827 were educated in special canton schools for future military service; after 1827 the term was applied also to Jewish boys, who, according to a statute issued on September 7, 1827, were drafted to military service at the age of twelve and placed for their military education in canton schools in distant provinces. The sons of Jewish soldiers were at this period regarded as government property and were educated for military service by the authorities, who, during the reign of Nicholas I, had a special regard for the Jewish cantonists, as it was easier to convert them to the Greek Orthodox Church than it was to convert their elders, whose religious principles had been firmly established. The best method to obtain this result was to take them far away from their birthplace so that they could forget their religion and be unprotected against the missionary propaganda of army officers. Eyewitnesses have many times described the torments endured by these innocent conscripts. The canton school was abolished in 1857 by Alexander II. For more information, see http://www.jewishencyclopedia.com/articles/3989–cantonists.

letter of introduction to a rich relative, asking for her help if it turned out that we could not find a way to support ourselves.

We traveled by train. Although my father did not look as though he was seriously ill, he spent the whole journey lying down. Our car was full of passengers, including a Jew from Starodub by the name of Liberman. Taking an interest in Father and learning that we wanted to put him in the hospital but, in all likelihood, as poor people from the provinces we would not be able to make this happen, he promised to help. According to him, one of his close relatives had influence with the hospital. Liberman gave us his address and told us to look him up if we found ourselves in need.

We arrived safely in Kiev, went to the address we were given, and, because of our inexperience, starting asking what to do. We were told that Kiev had a Jewish hospital. It was called the Brodskii Hospital.[57] This hospital was maintained by rich Jews for poor ones. In the springtime it fills up with sick people from all over Russia, because not everyone has the money to pay for a train ticket, and in the spring they can travel by river, which is much cheaper.

Before going to the hospital, we went to see a doctor. The doctor was so rude that I will never forget it. When my father turned away to get his money, and I stretched out my hand for the prescription, the doctor rudely shouted, "Pay me first." We found out from him what to do next and went to the Jewish hospital. Let me describe it. A beautiful entryway, like the entryway to a good park. Whole sections of the hospital for various illnesses. An endless number of sick people. People with incurable diseases weren't accepted as patients. They lay right there on the dirty floor, moaning, screaming, in torment. The people accompanying them paced the room in despair. What could be done with patients like that? They wouldn't make it home, and here there was no place to stay and nothing to live on. In that room I saw endless Jewish need and despair!

The so-called waiting room looked like an enormous railway station, dirty and full of tobacco smoke. There were few benches. Sick people, as I said, were lying on the floor. Ragged, tormented Jews had apparently lived their entire lives in endless need. Compared to these unfortunates, Father and I looked happy. People surrounded us, asking for alms, and we were ashamed to say that

---

57 Izrail' Markovich Brodskii (1823–1888) was a Russian sugar magnate and philanthropist. His gift of 165,000 rubles constituted the lion's share of funding for the hundred-bed Jewish hospital constructed in the new Luk'ianovskii District of Kiev. Treatment and medicine were free to both inpatients and outpatients. In 1908 the Brodskii Hospital treated 3,271 inpatients and 25,821 outpatients." See "Kiev," 9:529; and Meir, *Kiev, Jewish Metropolis*, 217–20.

we ourselves had nothing. We had to give to them, because there was no such thing as a stranger among them. By the time it was our turn to see the doctor, my nerves had been shattered by this scene, the likes of which I had never before encountered. When he had examined my father, the doctor said that we had to go home, because there were no places in the hospital. Nothing we said did any good, and we returned to our apartment.

We started thinking about what to do next. We decided to turn to the man from the train, Liberman, who had promised to help. We also decided to look up our relatives, whose addresses we didn't have. Father couldn't stand because of severe pain in his leg. As it turned out later, this was a complication of his illness. So it was my lot to become acquainted with such a big city as Kiev under terrible circumstances. Walking along the streets, I asked for directions. People looked at my clothes the way city people look at someone from the country. I pretended that I didn't understand. I couldn't care about their sneers. I sensed that my situation was terrible, but I tried not to fall into despair so as not to lose everything.

In the courtyard where we were staying was a Turkish bakery with a lot of workers. I was so afraid of them that I stopped crossing the courtyard on my own but waited until someone came. If, on the street, I asked a young man for directions he would look at me in such a vile way that I started only asking women.

The city was beautiful. A lot of greenery. People on the street were well-dressed. There were trams. People rode in fancy carriages. Couples walked arm in arm, at a time when it wasn't considered proper for a man to touch a woman's arm in public. People were unfriendly, mean. To find something out, you had to ask one person after another. Shop owners wouldn't miss even the smallest opportunity to make a sale. If you wanted change for ten kopecks, you had to buy something; otherwise they wouldn't give you change. In a word, compared to our people, these were beasts.

Although I found Liberman's address, I was afraid to enter at first. It was a big house on Kreshchatik, belonging to a certain Roshal´—the owner, as I later found out, of workshops that made things from gold. The doorman took one look at me and didn't want to let me inside, but I myself was afraid even to look inside. I walked up and down and in circles, until by chance I saw Liberman himself. Either he had really forgotten about our meeting or he regretted his promise, but he pretended he didn't recognize me. Finally remembering, he took me into the mysterious—as it seemed to me then—palace. When I entered these chambers, the luxury and wealth I saw there stopped my breath.

My heart contracted with anger. Why must my father lie sick because of his poverty, along with the thousands of Jews I saw in the hospital who had no idea why they were still alive and what awaited them, at the same time as such well-fed, healthy, rich men did no work and lived in luxury?

I was taken into a big room with furniture of red wood, apparently mahogany. There was luxury on the walls: the wallpaper itself, the portraits, paintings, chandeliers, carpets, busts, and various sculptures riveted me. I had hardly gotten a good look at the room when someone appeared at the door and said, "If you please!" Now I entered an even more luxurious room, done in black. Why it was black I didn't understand, but it was exceedingly gloomy. This was the study. The trim on the black was all silver and gold. In various places sparkled precious stones. The unusual surroundings made me speechless, unable to put words together. When Liberman found out why I had come, he promised to get Father into the hospital. As I left, I gave the doorman some money so that he would let me in the next day.

When I arrived the next day, Liberman told me that he had found out from the hospital that my father had stomach cancer and that the untreated cancer had progressed, so that it was too late to operate; that was why he had not been admitted into the hospital and would not be, because people whose diseases were incurable were not admitted. When I got home, I told Father that he had not been admitted because there weren't any openings. He understood everything right away and, sighing, said that we had to go home. Since he had relatives in Kiev, he wanted to see them before our departure. We had the address for one set of relatives but not any others, and I found them only with great difficulty. True, they were very responsive and came to see us right away. I also visited the relative from Auntie's letter of introduction, Mogilevkina. No matter who we saw, everyone was rich compared to us. Mogilevkina made a particularly strong impression on me. A large, beautiful, nicely furnished apartment. At the table sat her well-groomed son, a boy wearing a uniform with gold epaulets. As Mogilevkina explained later, he was a student at some university. She didn't even deign to introduce me to him, so as not to diminish her status in his eyes on account of her poor relatives. I was seized with anger and at the same time envy, because he was a student and could get nothing but Cs and was given everything he could possibly need, while I studied so well but had to become a tailor and live a life of piteous need and, to make matters worse, turn up in a big, unknown city where Jews weren't allowed to live with a sick father, without money, wondering every minute whether I would get him home alive. At every step I cursed the day of my birth and came to the conclusion that only rich people should have children, because poor people get only suffering from them and the children also suffer. When I gave Mogilevkina Auntie's letter, she wanted to know all about her, of course, but asked almost nothing about Father. If I hadn't needed her, I would have left immediately, but I had to get money from her, and she started to bargain with me to save Auntie some rubles. In the end I could bear it no longer, and I said that I was going to make an appointment for Father with Professor Wagner, since it would be wrong to leave without seeing such a luminary as Professor Wagner.

When I finally got to Professor Wagner's office, his doorman said that a consultation cost twenty-five rubles and that the first opening would be in two weeks. I was stunned, because we didn't have the money to stay in Kiev another two weeks. Then, against my wishes, I asked Mogilevkina to come with me to the steward, give him some money, and persuade him to get Father an earlier appointment. She didn't refuse, and we got an appointment for two days later.

In Kiev I learned about life in all its ugliness. Life there in those days was relentless. People cut each other's throats for money. Poor girls fell into the hands of rich scoundrels, after which they ended up on the street or in houses of prostitution. When, shortly after my arrival, I asked an older man how to get to some street, he gave me a brazen smile and named a certain house, saying, "Probably that's your destination." Of course, I didn't understand what kind of house that was, but his face filled me with fear, and I ran from him. When I told Mogilevkina about this, as we drove past those houses on the way to the professor, she pointed them out to me and explained in detail what they were. On the outside they looked the same as other houses, except that they were painted red. The windows were curtained. Nobody could be seen in the courtyards. By the stairs of one house stood a group of young girls, well-dressed but in maid's uniforms, with white bonnets and aprons, smiling brazenly at passersby. As Mogilevkina explained, now, in daylight, everybody was sleeping, and at night these houses were lit up with red lanterns and depraved men, particularly rich men, congregated here and squandered their money.

Every time I returned home, I found my father in a state of complete despair. He wept outright, fearing that during my long absences something had happened to me in that mad onslaught of people, where chaos reigned day and night.

Let me briefly describe our apartment and our hosts. The people we stayed with were old Jews, a husband and a wife. In the daytime they worked in the apartment, but they slept in Podol. This was a town outside Kiev where Jews were permitted to live. That Podol was so full of Jews that there was nowhere to find lodging for the night. There were times when people worked late, and at night they would hunt down Jews as though they were hunting wolves. Then they would march them in huge groups, like prisoners, back to the Pale. Among our neighbors were a husband and wife, and the wife had a residency permit but the husband didn't, or the other way around. It was pitiful to see in the evening how the father or mother would say goodbye to the family and go to Podol to sleep. It made a strong impression on me. Why were Jews persecuted like this? You'd often see a drunk lying on the street, of whatever nationality, and he had the right to live wherever he pleased. Yet the miserable, hungry, ragged Jewish beggar in search of a living had no rights at all. He was marched off like a criminal, and on his path he went through all the waystations and prisons.

Worst of all was the fate of Jewish girls. Some wanted to study, and others to work, but the government refused to let them, because they wanted to engage in honest labor. Instead of that, they were offered a "yellow ticket," a document held by licentious women, after which, on certain days, they would have to submit to an examination.[58] Such are the heights attained by Russian civilization! What an honorable girl was not permitted was possible for a licentious one. There were more than a few honorable girls who made use of this document to live outside the Pale of Settlement and nonetheless led worthy, honorable lives. That's one of the things I learned. I could write a lot more, but you can never record everything.

During the time that we lived in the apartment, there were a number of raids that our host found out about before they happened. He would send us out to the street. One day there was an unexpected shout: "Raid!" What should we do? I myself could dash out, but there wasn't time to get Father ready. What should we do? What if they took him away? They wouldn't make allowances for his illness, and he would die before he got to the nearest police station. I threw myself from one part of the room to another as though I'd been poisoned. Then our host appeared and said that he himself would take responsibility for Father, but I should leave the apartment immediately. As I reached the courtyard, I saw policemen heading to our apartment. I anxiously paced around the building waiting to see if they would take my father with them when they left. Each minute was an eternity. Finally they left, marching a group of Jews ahead of them, but my father wasn't with them. I rushed into the apartment. Father was lying there, terrified. He, poor man, was not worried about himself but about me. I calmed him down and asked what had happened. He said that the

---

58 Yellow tickets were issued to prostitutes.

host had curtained him off with a sheet and told him to cover his head. When the policeman asked who was there, the host answered that it was a woman in labor. The policeman took a look, and since he couldn't see a man's face, he left. Apparently he and the host had an agreement not to bother sick people.

The day came for the appointment with the professor. Father understood his hopeless situation. As we sat in a park waiting our turn, Father, laying his beautiful curly head on my lap, started to talk. He was worried about what would become of my brother Abram, who was only thirteen. He felt that I had already become a person, but he felt sorry for Abram. I was very surprised that he was worried only about Abram, when there was my little brother too. Why did he not say a word about him? How many times had I sent him presents? I thought he should have started heder. I had asked Father about him so many times, but he avoided answering. Now I asked, "Why aren't you worried about him?" There was no answer. I looked at him and saw heavy tears on his pale, thin face. I understood that my brother was no longer among the living and asked Father when he had died. I promised him I would stay calm and not cry. And at that moment I didn't know what to cry about first, the death of my little brother or the fact that my father was dying so young, without having seen anything good in life. Whatever had happened, he had been both father and mother to me. And I was about to be a complete orphan. When Mother was dying, I didn't understand all the horrors of life, the way I did now. It is hard to describe with a pen how heavy my heart was then. My father, crying, told me what had happened to my little brother. It turns out that he died a few days after I left for Khotimsk, around 1907. He came down with measles, because there had been no one to look after him. They opened the window by his bed, and he caught cold. He developed encephalitis and died. When I was with him he had been sick with diphtheria, and I, still a child, had brought him through, and here grownups didn't pay attention and a healthy child perished. In conclusion, Father said that since the child died he had had no joy from life and that he apparently would be seeing him soon.

Our turn came. When we found ourselves in the professor's study, the unusual surroundings frightened me. A big room, with a big table in the middle. Doctors were seated at the table. Professor Wagner himself, tall and heavy, looked the way someone of his profession should. Examining Father, he made a diagnosis and asked the doctors who were present to examine him as well. They spoke in Latin and wrote something in a book. Then he turned to us and said that we should go home, and he would give us medicine to take with us. When we left the study, the professor called me back. Asking what my relation was to the patient, he told me that the situation was hopeless: the cancer had progressed. If we had come even a month earlier, it would have been possible to operate, but now we needed to go home immediately. Going out to my father, I put on a brave front despite the two blows I had just received. But Father understood. Returning to the apartment, we prepared for our departure. We didn't have enough money for the train, so we had to go by boat to Gomel´. Traveling took a long time. We arrived safely in Klintsy. Father pleaded to be taken to Khotimsk, but the doctors advised against it, not certain that he would survive the trip. This was the spring of 1909. As he still did not look too sick, Auntie rented a cottage for him, and we spent whole days together in the woods. But this didn't last very long. His condition worsened, and we went back to Auntie. Soon his condition deteriorated sharply. That night I dreamed that my late mother was waking me up and saying, "Today your father will die, and you will be alone. Look after your brother." In the morning Father sent me for the doctor and asked for a prayer book. Not suspecting anything, I left.

When I returned, the courtyard and the house were full of people I didn't know. I was surprised, but when I entered the room I recoiled in horror. Father was lying on the floor (according to Jewish tradition, a dead person is taken off the bed and placed on the floor until being carried out). Unable to believe what had happened, sobbing, I threw myself on my dead father and lost consciousness. I came to in one of Auntie's rooms. Women surrounded me and comforted me. I didn't believe that he had died. I had fed him not long ago. So he understood that he was about to die and didn't want me to be present. Father died so young, at forty-three. From that moment Abram and I were complete orphans. Many relatives arrived, and the time came for the body to be carried out. I was called to say farewell to Father, as up to that time I wasn't allowed to sit near him. When they started carrying him out, I threw myself toward him, wanting to accompany him to the cemetery, but the men held me back. Even today I remember that I was not at the cemetery. Why didn't they let me go? Apparently they felt sorry for me. So ended the life of my poor father.

Let me return to my own life.[59] When I went to Klintsy in 1908, as I have already written, a young man made my acquaintance in a manner that didn't please me. It turned out that he had come to Klintsy for a short time, even though he was from Klintsy; he was working in Starodub because of his father's illness. Even though he was an artisan, my relatives talked of no one else. After

---

59 It is curious that the wrenching description of Doba-Mera's father's death is followed immediately by the story of her marriage.

we became acquainted he went back to Starodub but sent greetings through my girl cousins, who communicated them in a mocking way.

The summer passed; the time came for the autumn holidays, and the young man went home. He introduced me to his sister to make it easier for him to approach me. The whole week of the holidays I didn't work but went out walking every day. No matter where I went, everywhere, as if from beneath the earth, loomed this young man. People I knew exchanged glances and directed ironic comments in my direction, but I paid little attention. I didn't even think about him. When I was living with my father at the cottage, that young man, as a relative, had come to visit Father and was very attentive to him. He became a frequent visitor. I would see him to the door out of politeness. Once, after he left, Father asked, "Why is Iakov-Meisha's son visiting us?" That's what Father called him. I answered, "To see you." Then Father said that we had a lot of relatives, but nobody else visited. I shrugged my shoulders. "Which means," said Father, "that he's visiting you. I know that a lot of good young men have been interested in you, but he is the best of them; I like him. If he makes you a proposal, don't rebuff him. He gives the impression that he could grow into a devoted family man. Don't forget that you are a poor orphan. My days are numbered, and when I'm gone, your position will get worse. Today you are living with Auntie, and tomorrow Auntie won't want to support you anymore and you will have to wander from place to place. In addition, you'll have your younger brother Abram hanging around your neck, and you'll have to put him on his feet. Try to make him an artisan; then he'll be able to make a living. And you marry this young man."

This conversation left me very agitated. Yes, I tried to convince Father that I was still young and I still had time, to which he answered that nobody would take a girl without a dowry. After this conversation of ours, whenever our guest appeared I would feel awkward. Earlier I had behaved freely and easily with him, and now I became shy, kept silent more often, and couldn't explain to myself what was happening to me. That was the condition I was in when Father died. When I came to after fainting, our guest was standing by me with liquid ammonia. He was very worried about me and did everything he could to comfort me. When everybody went to the cemetery, he didn't want to leave me, but his father, understanding that people would start talking, took him along.

My life after Father's death. When everyone returned from the cemetery, I was the topic of conversation. One uncle announced that he understood that the young man was interested in me and that they should arrange a marriage with him, after which I would bring up Abram. I remembered my father's wise words about how we would be strangers to everyone. His feet were barely cold, and they already wanted to get us out of the way. The conversation upset me tremendously, and I left the room in tears and sat down in the place where, so recently, my father had been lying. I sat for many hours with my eyes glued to that spot, until they found me and took me away. After that evening I sat there every day, in the corner opposite the bed where Father had been lying, until my disappearance was noticed. Finally they locked the door to that room so I couldn't get in. Only then did I begin to get used to my new situation. When acquaintances saw me, they took me for my cousin, so much had I changed.

I sent Father's things to Khotimsk and then went there to get my brother Abram. Father had left property: the old house. There were four of us: my stepmother with a year-old daughter [Meita—MB] and my brother and I. My stepmother took the child and went to her family, and I took Abram to live with me—that is, with Auntie. I knew that she would not support both of us. To make matters worse, Abram had come down with food allergies. So I took him to Klintsy, but in my mind I was thinking, "The boy is sick and ragged, and I myself don't have a place to call my own. What do I do with him?" Every mile we got closer didn't bring me joy—on the contrary. I was better off here in the wagon. But despite my feelings, we arrived. My unsociable, frightened brother Abram wouldn't enter the house. He was ashamed in front of everybody and frightened. It took me a long time to convince him to step into the courtyard. I found him room and board not far from us, at eight rubles a month. I myself found a job not far from him with a kind boss, Liubimov, for fifteen rubles a month. The boss showed me respect, so I worked twelve hours a day for him, and afterward I took piecework home. In that way I paid for my brother's room and board and for his clothing.

Finding work for him was difficult. Following Father's wishes, I wanted to teach him a trade. My boss proposed giving him a seat at the table teaching him tailoring, but the family raised an outcry because they didn't want an artisan as their nephew. At that time nobody liked artisans. Counting on their help, I was afraid to oppose them and sent him for two years, unpaid, to the wealthy Rivin's big store that sold textiles and haberdashery. But Abram—downtrodden, fearful of people since childhood—became the scapegoat of the clerks. The bosses, true, valued his honesty, but the junior clerks feared that he would be an impediment to one or another of them in the future, so they undermined him in various ways and didn't teach him the job. He was very upset over this, and when he saw me, he complained and cried. I already regretted not having him taught a craft. The relatives in any case had already forgotten about him and didn't want to remember.

My life became harder. As I already said, Abram suffered from allergies. He needed to have his hair washed at least once a week along with a change of underwear. But where could this be done? Auntie forbade me to do it at her house. She was very fastidious about it, even declaring that if she found out that I had done this at her house, the next day I would have to find a new place to live. I didn't know what to do, where to turn. So I risked being thrown out of the house, and every Friday evening I would wait for him outside where he, poor child, would hide around the corner or behind a tree. When the whole house had fallen asleep, even the servant, because I was frightened even of the servant, who might tell, I had water prepared and I took him to my room. Trembling like a leaf, afraid that I might suffer because of him, he would whisper quietly, "What a good thing it is that our little brother died. And I should have died. So I wouldn't have to wander the streets like a stray dog, and I wouldn't be a burden on you." These words broke my heart, but worst of all was that when I washed him, dressed him, and put him on the floor to sleep (my floor was clean, but there was no other place, as he categorically refused to sleep in my bed), then, when I had put him to sleep, I didn't go to sleep myself because I had to wake him up at dawn, before people got up to put cows out to pasture, so that nobody would notice he was with me.

My God, how hard it was for me to walk up to the sleeping child who, after so much suffering, might be having good dreams, to wake him up and chase him into the street! I can't describe how many tears I shed over this. One day I couldn't hold out and fell asleep, and Grandma found him in my room. Abram turned white as death, grabbed his clothes, and got dressed in the courtyard, on the run. That's where Auntie saw him. Explanations began. I couldn't hold back my tears, which poured from my eyes in streams. In tears I explained that I knew that Father had asked her before his death not to leave us to the whims of fate. "I don't know if you promised him or not, but do whatever you want. I can leave right now, if you order me to. I am the sister of this unhappy boy, and it is my duty to be a mother and a father to him. It's not his fault that I'm not a good support, if I don't have a home to call my own." Auntie left without saying a word. And I continued in the same spirit, and once a week I washed Abram in my room and changed his clothes.

Time passed. The young man started to visit me. Everybody liked him. I liked him too, but life had turned me into a mistrustful, frightened little bird. Fate had been unkind to me from birth. Nobody had ever been genuinely kind to me, and so I never felt affection toward anybody. Life had taught me to fear everybody: not to lie but not to speak the truth, and that it is better to keep silent about what you know. I even avoided being with people. When a girlfriend came by, I would get dressed and go out for a walk, but most of the time I spent working or reading.

Auntie's clerk was Motia Poliakov, who had also lost both mother and father. He was our relative, the same age as I was.[60] When he was free, he would come to my room and share good news and bad. Of course, he had about as much good news as I did. I cheered up with him, and I stopped feeling so lonely in this big house. I was not needed, but Motia was; he was a clerk in a store, and he was paid, but he also suffered from loneliness. Gradually we became friends, like brother and sister. Of course, he couldn't help me with anything, but I could talk things over with him, and I knew he wouldn't tell. People noticed our friendship and attributed a different meaning to it, but neither he nor I thought that way, I in particular never had a thought like that. My view of life at the time was such that I wasn't interested in young men at all. I had lost my faith in people and my hope for a better life.

Even though I was always tired when I returned home from work, I was happy when my little brother came and told me how he spent the day. I would check to see that he was clean. Then Motia would come in, and my cousins. The young man would come also, and the room would be transformed into a cheerful gathering of young people. Even Grandmother, who loved to be around cheerful young people, would also appear often. It would happen that Auntie would come in, spend some time with us, and then, fearful of compromising herself, would leave. I myself got little pleasure from these gatherings. That is, on the outside I appeared happy, but my heart was heavy and empty.

But then there came an hour that roused me from my stupor: my acquaintance declared to me the goal of his visits and asked me to tell him whether or not I agreed to his proposal. Struck by this unexpected turn of events and unable to find words, I said I would ask the advice of Grandmother and Auntie. Of course, he was offended by this answer and said that when a person likes someone, there is no need for advice. I understood that he was right, but since my life had taught me not to trust anyone, I didn't love anyone and was afraid

---

60 Here and in other places, we see that against the background of very traditional shtetl relationships and behavioral norms there existed a parallel track that was much more permissive: he went into her room, she bathed her brother on Friday night, and so on. Motia Poliakov remained Grandmother's friend until extreme old age. I used to meet him at family funerals in the 1960s and 1970s.—MB.

of the thought that I would fall in love with someone and then turn out to be deceived. If at times in relation to some young man or other my young girl's soul would awaken, I chased these thoughts away and trembled from fear. Could a poor girl even dream of mutual love? A girl was loved if she grew up in happy circumstances, if she had parents and, in addition, a dowry, but why would anyone love me? I didn't have one or the other, the only thing they'd want would be to deceive me. Such were my thoughts when I saw that a young man wanted to make my acquaintance or spend time with me. When I saw or people told me that somebody was interested in me, I would become very afraid and avoid meetings. And that was why I answered the young man's proposal in this way. Not having parents, I did indeed tell Grandmother and Auntie that the young man who had been coming to visit for some time now—our relative, Medvedev, Meilakh the son of Iakov-Meisha—wanted us to go to America together, as we were both artisans. Here labor was very cheap, but there it paid better. Here I had no ties, no family, and we could bring my brother over later.

Hearing me out, Grandmother and Auntie gave their agreement but said that because he had not yet reached draft age, there was a danger that I could be spending four years alone. To the question of whether I would risk abuse because I was a poor orphan, Auntie answered that he was an honorable person and that she could see that he loved me sincerely and understood my position. I listened to my relatives. In addition, I remembered the words of my late father, "Don't rebuff him. He is a good person. He will take the place of a father and mother for you." But my heart was full of anxiety. What if his relatives didn't want a girl with no dowry? Oh, if only I could have pressed myself to my mother's bosom and asked her advice; how much would I have given for that! God, how difficult it was for me! Although I gave my agreement, my heart remained cautious. In case anything happened, I didn't want to blame myself. I tried not to go walking with him any place where there were few people; I tried on various pretexts to meet less often. He often reproached me for this, but it did not bother me much.

The summer passed. He was without work. It was decided that we would start making plans to leave. Gradually I learned that he had a big family, and they lived poorly. To my question of whether his parents knew about his decision and how they felt about it, he answered that they knew and approved. But people told me differently. They said his family saw it as nothing more than a young man passing time with a girl and that they would not allow him to marry so young and not in any event to a girl without a dowry. Of course, this upset me, and I cried endlessly.

At this time one of my aunts proposed a match with a different Medvedev, the old and wealthy bachelor Aizik, who, by chance, had just been introduced to me, for what purpose I did not understand. Of course, I rejected him and his money and would have been happy to reject my old acquaintance as well, as our relations had brought me nothing but worry and grief. Finally, at my insistence, Meilakh announced to his parents that we were leaving the country and asked their approval for our marriage. His father said he would like to have a talk with me first. I agreed, although the purpose of the conversation was not clear to me.

The conversation began with a question: why was I taking their son away and making him go to America? I answered that it was his idea. Then the father demanded that I promise not to leave the country, so that his son would also not leave. I, with my habit of obeying my elders, made this promise, even though I had no right to decide this question without my fiancé. When I told him about the conversation, he was shocked and said, "It doesn't matter that you promised. We'll go in any event, because it will be hard for us to find work here." I answered that I would not go back on my word and had no intention of defying his parents under any circumstances.

And so the America question was abandoned, which meant he had to find work. They decided he should leave. Their main goal in this was to send him away from me in the hope that he would forget me, but when love is true, people don't forget each other no matter how far away they are.

Meilakh decided to head toward Khar'kov, but at that time Jews did not have residency rights there. He got himself some kind of documents and prepared to leave soon after the autumn Jewish festival of Succoth. During the festival days I didn't work. My unofficial fiancé started insisting that we get engaged. This is according to Jewish religious tradition: in front of people, the prospective bride and groom make promises to each other and declare themselves engaged. I agreed on condition that his parents give their consent and be present. But his parents categorically refused. My fiancé was in despair. His parents' thinking went like this: Why tie him down? Let him go a free man, and maybe he will find a rich bride there. My fiancé, in tears, begged Auntie and Grandmother. He thought differently from his father. He was afraid to travel without being engaged, because he loved me truly and feared my indifference to him. Trying to persuade me, he said, "You don't need my parents. What role do they have to play here? You don't have parents, so assume that I don't have any either, if they mock my feelings in this way." But I insisted, and he left unencumbered.

After my fiancé left, I breathed a sigh of relief. I had already more than once regretted that I had become a fiancée and must feel myself under obligation and wonder about my future; in addition, I was burdened by his parents' attitude toward me.[61] What disturbed me so much was their unwarranted hatred of me, as I was not used to that from others. Even in places where nobody needed me, as a person people respected me and even loved me.

My life again progressed without anxiety and worry. I worked as before. After work, the young people of our household gathered in my room, or once again I would read. The autumn and half of the winter passed without my noticing. My fiancé, of course, did not forget me; he wrote often, even warmly, although not a single letter arrived without Motia Poliakov reading it, as he was the one who got the mail. But this didn't bother me; even his jokes at my expense didn't disturb me. Offended by his parents, my fiancé hardly wrote to them, although he wrote to me often. If my letters to him got held up somewhere, then telegrams would fly to me, or I would get such terrifying letters that even now, when I remember, I feel terrified.

Nonetheless he did not stay away but returned at the beginning of 1910. The only thing that made me happy about his return was his health and well-being. I had already gotten used to my former girlish freedom, and I wasn't ready to part so soon with my lonely but still girlish life. But there was nothing to be done. Once having given my consent, I had to follow through.

The next question was how. He had no job. He was young. The draft was ahead of him. And I had nothing. No help was to be had from anywhere. In addition, it would not be good to marry without his family, and they absolutely would not give consent. When they did at last agree, they demanded a dowry from Auntie of around three thousand rubles. Of course, Auntie had no intention of giving me that kind of sum. Then they forbade him to see me in the hope that Auntie would not permit our relationship to fall apart and would produce the money. But Auntie wasn't thinking that way. Personally I could not find any excuses for myself. I could not forgive myself for my conduct. Why had I become engaged so young? Hadn't I lived through enough before that? I was terribly frightened of his family. Despite my youth I understood a lot about life. If his parents couldn't separate him from me now, that was because he was very interested in me. But once we had been married for a while, and there was nothing to live on, they would lure him away. Then my life would be sheer torture, and that was precisely what I feared.

---

61 Though they were not formally engaged, Doba-Mera felt the obligations of that position.

I decided to leave Klintsy forever and end the engagement. When my fiancé found out about this, he started insisting that we marry without his parents' consent; that we just travel to the nearest railway station, get married, go to see them, and then, like it or not, they would have to accept it.

But I didn't want that. On the one hand, I didn't want to make them distraught. On the other hand, I knew that some very honorable young men were interested in me and that their parents would be happy to have me as a daughter-in-law, even without a dowry. I understood that not having a dowry was a terrible thing for a girl. But I didn't let my spirits fall because I had begun to earn well, and I had started to dress well, and I hoped that in a few years I would have a dowry and I could get married in a way that would be public, not in secret from the groom's parents. I stood firm on this point. That is, I gave my fiancé an ultimatum: either I would leave and then marry him when I had earned enough for a dowry, or he had to convince his parents to consent to our marriage.

Let me briefly describe his father's disposition and character, since I had by that time become slightly acquainted with him. He was a tall, handsome man with a big, heavy beard, well-built, a little severe-looking, determined, proud, and very energetic. Burdened with a large family, he worked long hours to feed his children. He liked, as I already said, to do things his own way and didn't take anyone else in the family into consideration. He was very intelligent, sometimes too intelligent.

Seeing that his young son was seriously in love but not wanting him to marry a girl without a dowry, he thought up a plan. He promised his son that he would agree to the marriage and that he and everyone else in the family liked me very much, and therefore he would invite me to stay with the family for a week or two. Because brides did sometimes travel far from home to visit their betrothed. "Together we'll prepare everything," [he said.] I didn't completely understand what was going on, but I had nobody to ask for advice. I asked Auntie, but she was already sick of everything: first, of my sufferings; second, of her fear that she would have to come up with a dowry; and third, people get married all the time without making a fuss about it, while with us literally the whole extended family got frantic. I personally was not happy with my life. The way things had turned out, staying is bad and leaving is sad.

To refuse my fiancé would be to destroy him, but going to live with his family would mean new torments for me. I understood his father perfectly well. He wasn't about to let us marry, and if I were to leave my own house, nobody would cast aspersions, but if I were to leave their house, then people would say bad things about me. But no matter how much I insisted, I ran up against my fiancé's pleading. He promised that if his father refused to marry us, he would leave with me.

As an inheritance from our father, we [i.e., Doba-Mera and her immediate family] had the little house. Four of us shared it: our stepmother with our stepsister, and my brother and I. The little house was next door to Uncle Alter's, and he very much wanted to own it. Through Aunt Gesia, the sister of his wife Lyfsha, he began asking me to sell it to him and then divide the money. As I hated Alter from childhood, I would have turned down the money despite my poverty and preferred that the house burn down to ashes, just as long as Alter was never able to use it. But then my stepmother appeared and insisted on selling, and if I refused, to give her her half, since she was in need. Auntie, of course, wanted Alter to have the house, so she gave my stepmother money in return for a note saying that she had received her part of the inheritance. Auntie then told me this: "If you want to live in Khotimsk, then pay me back, but if you don't, then the property can only go to Alter." Of course, I had no intention of creating a life in Khotimsk, but I had no desire to give the house to Alter when he didn't deserve it.

My fiancé and I decided to have the title for the property rewritten in my name and to see what it was like, whether it would be possible to build a life there. Actually it was clear to me that young people like us would have nothing to do there, but he hadn't seen it, and so we went. If we weren't intending to live there, then we could sell to the person who made the best offer, then repay the debt to Auntie. When we arrived in Khotimsk, we undertook to do this. Alter immediately resisted us on the grounds that the house was his and he would not permit anyone to sell it. Letters flew to Auntie in Klintsy. Auntie opposed me and said that if I didn't sell the house to Alter, first she would never let me past her threshold, and second she would send Alter documents that would ensure that nobody would buy it from me. It wouldn't have been an easy matter to sell the house in any event, especially when a bad neighbor was right there defaming us. At that time only Jews would buy. What kind of Jew would buy himself a place to live and start a fight with his next-door neighbor? Getting a letter like that, I cried bitterly, bitterly. Now I had lost everything. At a time when I had nothing and nobody, people wanted to steal the last thing I had to live on. [The five lines that follow are crossed out.—MB]

At this point I understood that the only person who was interested in me and devoted to me with his whole heart, without calculation, was my fiancé. We transferred the property to my name but decided to wait on selling, since on account of Alter there were no appropriate buyers, and we didn't want to sell it to him for next to nothing. We returned to Klintsy: my fiancé went home; I went to Auntie's. My relationship with Auntie deteriorated. My fate was being decided. It was out of the question to continue living with her. I could either seek my happiness in some other place or give in to my fiancé and marry him at the first opportunity. So that is what I did. I took my things, hired a driver, and my fiancé and I went to his family. It took me time to get ready because I was so afraid of this step; it was the decisive step that would set the course of my entire life. I went as though condemned to death. I cursed the day of my birth and my father's unhappy inheritance that deprived me of my last little refuge and of my hope.

I delayed because I was hoping that somebody from the family would ask me to stay. But that didn't happen. When the servant told them [that I was going], they didn't leave the room. As I was on my way out, I wanted to say goodbye to them and thank them at least for the kindness that they had shown me up to this point. When I wanted to enter their rooms, the servant said that the mistress wasn't home. I said my goodbyes to the servants. They all cried, and with a broken heart I cast a farewell glance at my empty room with its empty bed, where I had stayed for so long and dreamed many dreams that would remain unknown and unfulfilled.

I write these lines thirty years later. And everything I went through can't be described, because I have no time to do that. But, as if it were happening now, before me is the image of that dreadful life. Other people parade their youth, but I soaked every step in bitter tears. Although I'm already a grandmother, the thought of that life frightens me; it is hard even to write about it. I write, and tears, of their own will, flow from my dimmed eyes along my wrinkled cheeks and fall unnoticed onto the notebook. At such a moment I am overwhelmed by my past—that is, by all my sufferings that nobody cared about, how I was unneeded by anyone. How much health did I lose over this!

It is well-known that a person's life takes place in stages—that is, in periods of time. For example, childhood, youth, and so forth. As we know, I had nothing like a happy childhood; I hoped, that when I grew up, things would be good. But now I was already grown up; I had a fiancé and was thinking of getting married. Again nothing was good, and I saw nothing comforting in the future. We were both poor. There was no help or support to be had from anywhere. At that time girls like me often found themselves in hopeless situations. They often became the unhappy victims of rich people's fancies. That is what I feared. I firmly decided to struggle with difficulties, not to lose heart, and look at everything in an uncomplicated way. I hoped to overcome everything.

My life in his home—that is, the home of my fiancé and his parents. When we drove up to his parents' little house, the children streamed out onto the street to meet us. But the father and mother stayed by the window and smiled ironically at my dowry, as if to say: it all fit into a single wagon. My fiancé was very happy that day, but when I found myself in their house and each member of the family came up to me and looked me over and started asking me questions, even though they had seen me before and knew the answers, I got very nervous. It was Friday afternoon when I crossed their threshold. Only my fiancé and the little children were happy. The parents and the older children hid their dissatisfaction with me. In vain had I dreamt that the parents of my husband would take the place of my own parents. Here I understood that I had made a profound mistake. It was not only that they didn't like me. They hated me, and I didn't know why. If earlier, living with Auntie, I could sometimes sing and laugh, here that came to an end. I was seized with despondency.

Not a week passed before the whole city and all the relatives knew what kind of dowry I had brought. The father told this story to all and sundry in order to shame Auntie for sending me off without a dowry. Auntie didn't care, but I became very upset. A week passed, then another, and the father was still not doing anything about the marriage. I was afraid to talk to him, and when I spoke to my fiancé, he promised to do it, but I understood that he was also afraid. Finally he had the conversation. Then the father, angered by this, categorically refused, saying that I had no connection to him, I was not his fiancée, and that it was only out of pity for me that he was letting me live with him. This answer startled us, and I, choking down tears, came out, and my fiancé told him that I was his fiancée and he wanted no other, and that if he did not consent to marry us, we would go to some place nearby and get married. My fiancé followed me out of the house, and we set off to the city to get advice on our next step. We had hardly gone a block when we heard his father shouting from behind. Untroubled that people could hear him, he cursed as he called his son back to the house. But my fiancé didn't want to go. I understood that he was afraid. Still I insisted that he go home, and I myself decided: if he didn't name a wedding date right now, we would marry without him, find a room, and begin our life [together]. I didn't return to the house but waited in the spot where my fiancé had left me. I waited for a long time. He emerged distraught and announced that they would not consent and we must prepare to marry without them.

On the way to the city lived my cousin Girsh Medvedev. He had a very intelligent wife who respected us very much. She wanted to end our sufferings as soon as possible and helped us with a lot of advice. To this day I respect her greatly for what she did. After the final refusal from his parents, we turned to her first to tell her what had happened and ask her what to do next. I understood that the parents had deceived me and waited for their son to reject me. Instead, the more they tried to set him against me, the more he loved me and pitied me.

After talking with our relative Khana [Girsh's wife—MB], we came to the same conclusion and left them for the city. After our departure, when my fiancé's father passed by their house, Khana stopped him and gave him a tongue-lashing on my behalf. She announced in no uncertain terms that if they did not arrange our wedding, then she would do it, because they had deceived me, an orphan, and I had nobody to take my side. When he heard that I had defenders, he announced that our wedding would take place during the autumn holidays.

Can I possibly describe the extent to which his family harassed me? I don't blame them as much as the father, the head and terror of the family. The children all trembled in fear at his very appearance, and the family followed his example in everything. When I asked him when the wedding would take place, he asked in surprise, "To whom am I marrying my son? This girl, who lives with me—I took her in out of pity for a poor orphan." His words cut me to the quick, because I didn't deserve them. I didn't thrust myself on them. To the contrary, I didn't want to offend them in any way.

Sometimes they would see me reading a book aloud, and for a moment the children would forget their hatred of me, sit around me, and ask me to read aloud. I wasn't a bad reader. All the children would gather around and listen to me with pleasure. But no sooner would the father appear at the threshold, then they would run away in fright, heading in whatever direction they could. Sometimes he would appear unnoticed, and everybody would be absorbed and not see him. Then, after standing there for a short time, he would abruptly say to one of the children, "Now you read. You read better. You can't understand her or make out what she is saying." And he would take the book out of my hands and give it to his chosen one, and the child, alternately blushing and turning pale, would put a finger on the page and read syllable by syllable. He, satisfied, would nod his head and approve the reading, and the children gradually, little by little, would abandon the reader, and I would obey silently, and my heart would contract from the humiliation. Or one of the children would say, "Today there's going to be a good play. We should go see it." I would say, "Of course," out of politeness. Then the father would say, "You don't have decent clothes. Some fiancée, she has no decent clothes. People have fiancées in their families, and they always have clothes." I had no words to answer him, and my heart was racing. Why was it my fault that I had little? I had no parents to support me, and I was too young to have acquired anything on my own. I wore what I had.

Finally the long-awaited time came—that is, the holidays—and we needed to prepare for the wedding. The father again thought up an excuse to break his promise, but under pressure from relatives he named a day for the wedding. Even though I myself wished an end to the uncertainty, when that day came I was very frightened. First, I was alone. Second, I understood that something very important was being decided in my life today. And that my fate depended on it.

On that day I fasted and went with my little brother Abram to Father's grave. Falling on his grave, I poured out all my sorrows in tears, and I imagined that Father heard but could not respond. For a long time I lay on his grave and sobbed and didn't even notice that my brother was asking me to go home. In those minutes nothing and nobody else existed for me but this deaf and mute grave. I would have preferred to stay here than return to people who hated me for no reason and enter a marriage with someone from this family. What unknown fate awaited me? My little brother Abram, seeing that I had already lost my voice from shrieking, called people who were at this time walking around the cemetery, and they dragged me off the grave and Abram took me home. Broken-down, hoarse, half-mad, I waited indifferently for the time of the wedding.

A few days before the wedding I had gone to my relatives to invite them. I also invited Aunt Gesia. She was no longer angry at me and gave me a lot of wedding presents, including new fabric for shirts. The wedding was to take place in a large house owned by relatives of the Zlotins.[62] The girls of the house, my relatives, tried very hard. Everything was put together in excellent taste. The chair where I sat was decorated with beautiful, real flowers, as was the wall in front of which we sat. The table was also decorated. Everything was very pretty, but it didn't make me happy. In fact, it frightened me. With what joy would I have fallen on my mother's breast and, sobbing, told her of all that had happened and asked how to overcome it. But whatever my thoughts, evening arrived. I was helped into my wedding dress. Many relatives came as guests, including Auntie and Uncle. Jews have a tradition that the bride is led to the

---

62 The Zlotins were the family of Meilakh's mother, Khaia-Reize (1870–1941), the wife of Iakov-Meisha. She was killed by the Nazis in Klintsy together with her two daughters and four grandchildren. Her name before marriage was Zlotina.

ceremony by her parents. If the parents have died, then she is led by a relative of their generation. When the moment came, my late mother's brother and sister took me by the hand. Oh! I will never forget that moment. This is when I needed my parents more than ever. Why was I punished so cruelly? If only one of them were alive! This moment was the most terrible of all for me. I was so struck by it, that in my exhaustion I fell, sobbing, onto the table, and everybody around me was crying their fill. Finally I was taken from my place and led forward. I didn't see anything and didn't understand what was happening with me.

I came back to life only when, seated at the table for the wedding supper, the merry guests started to congratulate me and the groom. I was drained and exhausted after such a difficult day. After the supper came the traditional dances, and it would have been awkward for me to turn down the invited guests, so I danced a little with them. The relatives gave us many presents. The rich ones tried not to spend so much, fearing for their savings. Aunt Gesia gave the most. On this occasion, despite everything, she acted more honorably than anyone else.

At long last, one stage of life had passed. The second one began. You get married only once in a lifetime. That is, sometimes it repeats, but then it doesn't play such a huge role in a person's life as the first time, especially for a girl. As soon as a girl begins to understand that she is a woman and that she will have to get married, she transfers all of her girlish hopes and dreams to her future companion, in the belief that he will be her future protector and defender. She doesn't think that this protector can become her greatest accuser and enemy. Cases like that happen often. This is because when men go courting, they hide or restrain their natures, concerned that their friends may lose respect for them. So they try not to reveal their true faces. But when the couple unites, the mask gradually starts to disappear, and it turns out that the two people are completely different in all ways. In such cases, the husband, considering himself the rightful boss of his wife, takes charge and starts doing whatever he wants with her, as though she were some kind of inanimate object. Then the wife, if she doesn't want to submit, makes scenes. At first behind closed doors, then openly, and the couple turns into wild beasts stuck together in a single cage, ready at the first opportunity to sink their teeth into each other's throats. Forgetting all propriety, and without regard for the fact that just a short time ago these people were trying hard to be together and believed that when they arrived in that unknown world, they would join together and be happy. When the woman is obedient, she begins by yielding to her husband and subordinating herself to him in everything, trying to hide his offenses against her as long as she can, and it looks as if their life is good. In the old tsarist days, nobody gave particular consideration to the woman, but even now she is far from equal with the man. I have already seen a great deal in life, and I have come to the conclusion that all men are egoists and despots with regard to their wives. It is so natural to them that they aren't aware of what they are doing and don't acknowledge it. They want you to pay the maximum attention to them, greet them and see them off tenderly, and serve them and pick up after them. And if he is annoyed with something, then he can scream at his wife for no reason, and she has to tolerate it. That is essentially the character of a man, even a man we consider to be a good husband. He doesn't stop to think if his wife can serve him and pick up after him. Maybe she is very tired. Let's say both of them work, and when she returns from her work, the wife is again at work, taking care of the children, and at the same time she serves and looks after her husband. I have never seen a husband share these duties equally with his wife. The husband considers this to be completely natural, the way it ought to be. For that reason, a girl's life is free of harm or hurt only until she marries. She may have lived well and she may have lived poorly, but either way she has no obligations to anybody, nobody gives her orders, and her heart isn't full of pain because of anyone, and however much she has it is enough, because she is alone.

Let me return to where I left off. And so we married. We returned to the home of his parents drained and exhausted. Instead of feeling joy because we had married after overcoming so many obstacles, we sat down to figure out our future plans. Before us stood the question of what to do. How should we start our life, and with what money? We had almost no money aside from the twenty-five rubles that Aunt Gesia had given us to buy a bed. We very much wanted to remain in Klintsy. We would have rented a room and gotten jobs, but since, to our misfortune, we had a little cottage in Khotimsk by way of the inheritance from Father, his father insisted that we move there, even though we didn't want that, and nobody advised us to do that. But how could we object?

I have already written that his father didn't take anybody's wishes into account, on the assumption that everything he did was correct. Therefore, against our will, we went to Khotimsk. There were renters in the house. They had promised us that when we needed it for ourselves, they would let us in. But when we arrived, they let us stay there for a few days, then went and threw all our things onto the street. That was the beginning of our new family life.

Out of respect for my late father, the people of Khotimsk stood up for us. They called an arbitrator, and we had to pay the tenants twenty-five rubles to rent a different apartment. Thus we began our new life without money. We had a lot of friends, sincerely devoted to us, but nobody could give us material help.

They nicknamed us "Love and Poverty." Of course, despite our poverty we lived very amicably. We did not reproach each other for our shortcomings. We were happy that we lived tranquilly. We both worked but couldn't earn enough to live on. A rich carpenter by the name of Alter-Turik gave us furniture free of charge. He said he didn't have anywhere to put it, anyway. We furnished the house like a little toy, but at times we simply had nothing to eat. Some people from Klintsy rented vegetable gardens in Khotimsk. One such person was an acquaintance of ours, and he found out that we were living poorly. Looking at us, you wouldn't necessarily know. Our house was clean, and we dressed neatly. But this gardener was a very clever old man, and when he found out, he started to supply us with vegetables and lend us money. Aunt Lyfsha next door would be looking to see if I lit the stove late on Friday, although that would be because before that I didn't have the money to buy [food for the Sabbath—MB].[63] The sun would go down, and I would have to go hungry that day and the next. She didn't ask why I was lighting the stove late but threatened that she would pour water on it. All the same, more than once we didn't eat, fearful of a scene from her, if we didn't have food to cook early enough.

But food was the last thing on our minds. We organized a group of young people who loved theater. We put on Gordin's *Khasye di yesoyme* [Khasia the orphan—MB]. I played Khasia, and my husband played Trakhtenberg. We acted well. There was a large gathering, and the money went to the Khotimsk Society to Aid Poor Jews. When the performance was over, people brought me many good things to eat. Toward the end of the last act, the audience tossed flowers at me. We weren't troubled that we didn't have money to live on. We were happy. Nonetheless, our material deprivation and all that I had suffered took their toll, and the next autumn I fell seriously ill. This was in 1911. At first it did not seem serious, but the longer it lasted, the worse it got, and I couldn't leave the bed. If before we had nothing to live on but we had our health, now I was sick. We needed a doctor, medicines, special foods. Where could we get these things? We started to borrow money, but I wasn't getting better. I spent all that autumn and winter in bed. Spring began. One day, somebody summoned

---

63 Jewish law prohibits lighting a fire and preparing food on the Sabbath, which begins Friday at sunset. For that reason, on Friday afternoon all unsold perishables at the market were highly discounted and poor people could afford them.

a doctor from Klimovichi. They brought him to see me too. He didn't have anything good to say. I was getting worse, and not a single doctor could say what the problem was. Once, when I was in a very bad state, the local doctor was sent for, and in my presence he said that my condition was hopeless and that if I lived until summer, I would have to go for a koumiss [fermented horse milk—MB] cure in Crimea. Nothing in this surprised me, as I was already fed up with lying in bed, tormenting myself and my young husband.

When the doctor left, my husband ran to me, sobbing, "Don't worry, I won't let you die. You must live." That night as I slept, my illness got worse. My husband kept vigil by my bed, noticed this, and woke me. When I awakened, I had lost the gift of speech and my sense of touch. I heard and saw everything, but I had become indifferent. My husband started to tug at me, yell and cry, beg me to say just one word. But I couldn't. My body was like a log; it couldn't be moved. In horror, he cried, "You're dying!" I will never forget his terrified face. But I was lying there and thinking, "Why don't people want to die? Nothing hurts me now. Why is he crying?" The only thing I badly wanted was to see my only brother before I died and tell him not to cry over me too much and that he should be a good person, to look at him one last time. Because I had nobody else, only my husband and my brother.

That was my condition, and my poor, tormented husband was just rushing around the room, with no idea how to help me. Every minute he pleaded with me to tell him what was happening to me and kept repeating that he wanted to die before me, that he wouldn't live without me. He wanted to run and get somebody to help, but how could he leave me on my own? Finally he left me and ran for Aunt Lyfsha's. When they finally answered his knock, instead of coming to do something, they said that it was out of their hands. Defeated, he ran into the street and saw two girls, servants who were sitting on a bench. He ran to them, asked them to stay with me, and himself ran for the doctor's assistant, as the doctor himself had asked not to be summoned any more.

When the girls caught sight of me, they started to cry. I thought this was strange. Or perhaps at that moment it was terrifying to look at me; I still don't know. Many times later I asked my husband what I looked like then, but he never answered.

My husband brought the doctor's assistant and he started taking my pulse, and then he did something to me. In a word, after some time had passed, I came to myself and started crying. I remember as though it were happening now the doctor's assistant saying she's yours, and if you hadn't awakened her, she would have died in her sleep. The doctor's assistant left, and I started to feel fine. Joyfully, my husband warmed up some tea, and we drank it together, and toward morning we fell asleep.

It won't hurt to include something about harassment from the side of Uncle Alter himself. From the first day of our arrival in Khotimsk, he did his best to force us out, to take possession of our "palace." He still wanted to possess our palace. When I got sick, it was winter and there were heavy frosts. It was cold in the house. The floor froze. We had to pile up soil around the house. That's the way wooden houses in the provinces were kept warm in the winter. But Alter wouldn't let us make piles along the wall that was in his yard. And that's where my bed was, in which I lay sick. People shamed him, cursed him, but he had no intention of giving permission. We were advised to go to the police chief; then they would force him. But how can you take your own uncle to the police? Of course, we didn't go, and we had to knock down part of the floor to make a mound on the inside. To do this, we had to bring in soil from outside, and the house became so cold that my illness got much worse. It's not surprising that when my husband went to them for help, they didn't respond. They were perhaps even happy at this turn of events.

After that terrible night, when we fell asleep only when it got light, and they needed to go somewhere, they—that is, my lovely uncle and aunt—woke us up and brought us five or six of their children. We were outraged by their presumption, given that they knew about the terrible night we had just had. But we didn't have the nerve to throw them all out and close the door on them once and for all. Of course, this day was very difficult for me—I had to spend it among little children. But I nonetheless started to get better.

Gradually I began to sit up, then walk, and finally I went outside. I looked terrifying. People stopped on the street to stare at me. This disturbed me a lot, and I began walking in our courtyard, so nobody would see me. It was decided to send me to doctors in Kiev, but in the meantime to Klintsy. And from there to Kiev. The weather was already warm, and I was put in a wagon and brought to Klintsy half-alive.

I arrived at the house of my husband's parents. I was lifted out of the wagon, and my husband's father, angry, said to his mother, "I said before that he shouldn't marry her, that she would be sick, and now he'll have to deal with a sick wife his whole life." Of course, he was right, but who made me so nervous? Who made us suffer from hunger in Khotimsk?

It was decided to consult Dr. Grebennikov. This was a doctor who told patients the whole truth right to their face, even if they were going to die soon. It was to him that we went. When he had examined me and asked about my parents, I decided that he was about to issue a death sentence. But it turned out otherwise. He didn't tell me to travel anywhere and advised me to eat well, not to worry, and to sit in the woods. He prescribed medicine.

But the weather was rainy, and I lived far from the woods. Most of the time I had to stay at home. My husband wrote his parents pleading letters that I was all he had, and if they had pity on him, to save me for his sake. He no longer concealed his love for me. He begged them, pleaded with them, in every letter. But they didn't like me. That was the first thing. Their selfishness did not allow it. In addition, they were poor.

But Auntie thought differently. She began to send me things to eat, in secret from my husband's father. She sent butter, eggs, cut-up chicken, meat, chocolate, and many delicious things. When the weather was good and I sat in the woods, she would send a delicious dinner, and I quickly regained my health.

But my husband's father didn't believe that I was getting better, and when he found an opportunity, he dropped in unexpectedly. I was frightened by his sudden appearance and fainted. My husband saw this and shouted, "Water! Water!" His father, cursing, said, "She wants to wipe you from the face of the earth. She wants to scare you. She's putting it on. She was just singing songs with the little girls." But my husband gave him a look, a look that said everything, forever. To which his father responded, "You are her husband, and according to Jewish law you are obliged to do everything for her, and if there is nothing to eat, then you have to sell your coat in order to support her, even if she doesn't deserve it, but I am not obliged."

At that time I needed complete rest, but every day I had to listen to various lectures, orders, and unjustified reproaches from his father, and I was afraid to open my mouth and say even half a word in my own defense. The only person in the family who understood me and took pity on me was my husband's sister Eidlia, who has since died. She was also forgotten by everyone in the family because she was quiet, meek, and inoffensive. She worked harder than everyone and was kicked around by everyone. Most important, my husband's father didn't like her at all. His favorite was Sima. She dressed better than everyone else and worked less. Eidlia was very hurt by her family, but she loved me sincerely and tried to protect me from anxiety. And I tried to spend time at Auntie's until the father came home, so as to forget the situation however briefly.

A month flew by, and I was much better. When I returned to my doctor, he was ecstatic over my condition. Now even more than before I did not want to go back to Khotimsk, where my whole life I had seen nothing good. And what awaited me there? I had hardly any relatives except Uncle Alter's family, who couldn't wait to see the back of me. But my husband's father said to go, and there was no way out of it. When I returned to Khotimsk in good health, my husband was afraid to let people see me, lest they invoke the evil eye. He hid me.[64] But friends demanded to have a look at me, and the poor fellow had to go back on his plan. Everybody was delighted at how healthy I looked, all the more so as they remembered what I was like when they saw me off.

Life resumed. It was the autumn of 1912. My husband faced the draft. He had a deferment, but sometimes, if there was a large intake, people with a deferment also got drafted. I was in despair, not so much because he would get drafted, but because if he did I would be left without family in a place where it would be impossible to make a living. But it was impossible to oppose his father, so we had to stay in Khotimsk. Finally my husband was called in, and he got his deferment.[65] When he returned home, I once again began to ask how long his father intended for us to live in Khotimsk. He answered that he himself didn't know, that he had spoken to his father about it, and that his father had categorically refused to allow us to leave Khotimsk.

There was nothing to be done: we stayed and suffered. The winter passed, and then the spring and most of the summer. We learned that his father had become seriously ill. In our letters we began to plead with him to allow us to return to Klintsy. Finally he did. We began looking for a buyer for our house, but Alter went back to his old tricks. He used various threats to prevent people from making an offer but himself offered half of what others were willing to pay. It was as if he took the house away from us. Finally his soul found peace: he had made us leave. But I was very happy that I was going to Klintsy, where I could earn a living. My youthful inexperience did not foresee how much worse it would be to live close to his parents, who hate me to this day. We should have left for any other city, where it would have been possible to find a job and be farther from his family.

August 1913. We arrived in Klintsy, and here's what we found. Grandpa was ill. The household was in need. We had to find jobs and a place to live. For the money we got from the sale of my father's house we could buy a place to live, but again our inexperience undermined us: the money was spent, and we were left with nothing. We rented a little room and a workshop. When we first arrived in Klintsy and my husband saw what was going on, he began to

---

64 A superstition that if, for example, you praise someone's beauty or health, you can inadvertently call forth misfortune on that person.
65 Apparently as a married man, who were drafted with the second intake.

withdraw from me. There were many reasons. First, someone had to go to Gomel´ to buy tools and other necessities for work. We decided to go together, but his father objected that he himself had never taken his wife anywhere, and he managed. My husband argued that I had never been anywhere, and that later I wouldn't be able to, as I was pregnant with our first child, Zaia. At this point I understood that I had gone from the frying pan into the fire. That here I would suffer all my life. And that's how it happened. The suffering that I endured until leaving for Leningrad is impossible to describe. My blood curdles in my veins when I recall even isolated incidents. In the whole world there is nobody more inhumane than his family was in relation to me. This was when they decided to pay me back for entering their family without their consent. Once again my inexperience and my inability to adapt to that kind of life worked against me. In addition, I was lonely. Who did I have to complain to? Who could help me? My God! To the whole world I was an unwanted stranger, and I myself could not find a solution. Every day brought me new suffering, even as yesterday's wounds were still fresh. New wounds that they inflicted on me. I swallowed my tears in silence and awaited the birth of my child. The autumn holidays came. His father demanded that we celebrate at their house. We went together. We arrived. My husband was surrounded. There were secrets that I wasn't privy to. We returned home that night. He ran ahead. He was angry. I started to stumble, I fell, I walked slowly, and he criticized me for falling behind. I went and swallowed my tears, not expecting anything better.

One day we left our apartment key at their house. When we got there and realized we had forgotten the key, my husband exploded at me despite the late hour and even though people were asleep and we were equally responsible. He did it even though he had loved me not long ago and people could hear, which was quite embarrassing. When we somehow got the door open, he continued to yell. Where did he get that vocabulary? So recently he had been kind and loving. What happened to that? How did I deserve this? I couldn't understand. I cried all night, until morning.

In the morning, when he went out to wash, I heard him talking with the owner of our apartment. The owner was Aizik Medvedev. He had once respected me and once was even interested in me, but he was eight years older than me and for that reason I didn't want him, which I later regretted more than once. He and his wife lived well, while I was beaten down by the grief of my unhappy fate. I heard him say, "What you want from her, Meilakh, I don't understand. People better than you were interested in her. You won. Which means you liked her. So why are you treating her like that? I see everything.

You are obeying your family. Then why didn't you obey them earlier and not marry her? You treat her badly because she has nobody to stand up for her. So understand, people like that will come along!" My Meilakh didn't say a word, just went and rented a different apartment. That evening we moved.

Let me describe the new apartment. If at Medvedevs' we lived surrounded by people, here our little house was in the garden. The courtyard was very long, and you got to the little house by way of the garden. It was low and looked like a bathhouse. Along the way, there was a house that was falling apart. It had belonged to an old tailor who buried children. If somebody's child died, he was called. He would take the child and bury it. People paid him for this. They said that if the weather was bad and he couldn't bury them the same day, he left them in this shed. When I found out about this, I became afraid to stay home alone.

Autumn evenings. Winds. Trees rustled, like the cry of a child. And I was alone with my frightening thoughts. My husband returned home late. After work he would go to see his family. Auntie Gesia, who had found out about our move and looked over our new living quarters, was very dissatisfied and protested strongly. She began looking for a new apartment for us and did not allow me to visit his family after Medvedev, our former landlord, told her what had happened and of my husband's poor treatment of me. Auntie found me my own apartment, consisting of a room and a kitchen. It was cheerful. Auntie lived next door, and she often sent her servant to help me, so that it would be easier for me in the last days (before the birth). This was at the beginning of December 1913.

My husband began visiting his family less often and started behaving better toward me. I don't know what caused this—his conversation with Medvedev or the fact that he visited them less often. In any case, I calmed down a little.

At the beginning of 1914, my oldest son Izrail´, Zaia, was born.[66] (When I started feeling pains, I sent my husband for the midwife, and he asked what kind of pants to put on, his everyday ones or his Sabbath ones.) His relationship with me improved. Here, under Auntie's nose, it was like living in the lap of Jesus. In the summer of 1914, my husband's father died. This was a truly heavy blow to the family. When I went to see them, he was lying dead, and it was a shocking scene. Nine children, of whom four were small—and of the

---

66 According to entries in a rabbinical record book, Izrail´ (Zaia)-Vel´ka Medvedev, the oldest son of Doba-Mera and Meilakh, was born on December 24 (9 Tevet), 1913. See GABO, f. 585, op. 1, d. 3, l. 223. According to the Gregorian calendar, this was the beginning of January 1914. Zaia died in St. Petersburg on November 11, 2001.

five older ones, only Malka and Eidlia were hardworking, something that the rest of the family resented. They had absolutely nothing to live on. The walls were bare. The children didn't have shoes or clothes, because of their father's long illness during which everything went for medicine. Since my husband was the oldest, they flew at him like vultures after their prey. "You're the oldest, it's your responsibility," [they cried.] But from everything that had happened, my husband himself came down with a respiratory illness and had to be sent away to recover.

First he went to see a professor in Kiev, then to a private sanatorium in Otvodsk, near Warsaw. This is easy to write or say, but how to make it happen, if the local doctors had issued him a death sentence? And I was without means, with a baby on my hands. I can proudly say that thanks to my persistence and to the respect people had for me, which I made use of, I managed to make it happen. Do you think it was possible in those days for people without means to dream of a sanatorium?

While he was in the sanatorium, the Serbian prince was killed and rumors predicted that war was inevitable.[67] My husband returned home without completing his course of treatment, but he had nonetheless gotten stronger and gained weight. I wasn't fated to get much joy from this. He needed to eat special foods and live in a country house surrounded by pine woods. With a tiny baby on my hands, I had to work day and night to provide for his food, not thinking about myself or the child. I remember how sometimes he would take Zaia into his arms and, weeping, tell him, "It won't be my lot to raise you. You won't remember Papa. Mama will tell you what he was like and how much he loved you." Can you imagine what I felt, hearing this?

I remember he spent some time in Pochetukha, in the woods. I made him dinner and kefir. To earn some money, I sold kefir to other dachniks who had dachas in the woods.[68] Can you imagine what it would be like to drag yourself uphill for two kilometers with a six-month-old infant in one arm and in the other dinner and bottles of kefir? I couldn't rest, because if I put down what I was carrying, I wouldn't be able to pick it up again. It's hard to describe the condition I was in when I reached the woods. My hair was a mess, my face was red, my throat was parched. But nothing was too hard for me if only he would get better. Only once in a while did he actually eat this food. Mostly it was because his family would come, knowing that he had good things to eat, and he would

---

67 Incorrect: an Austrian prince was killed by a Serb.
68 A *dachnik* is a person who rents a dacha (summer house).

not have the benefit of my labors. This distressed me a great deal. They were completely healthy and could eat the same things I ate. Nobody could imagine how I got these things, to start with, and there was nothing to replace them with, and it didn't occur to anyone that the issue was not dinner but saving his life. Despite all these difficulties, I managed to get him back on his feet. I remember how hard it was to get him to the point that he would eat something or drink a glass of milk or cream. As a rule I tried to put butter into the milk. I would put the milk in front of him and coax him. He would touch the glass and say, "It's too hot," then ask for it again and say, "It's too cold." So you'd hurry and warm it up. And the conditions under which I did this! To warm up the milk meant making a fire from twigs and heating it on a tripod. You'd heat it, and then the whole thing would start in again. Or he would suddenly get angry and refuse to eat or drink. It didn't help to tell him that we had a child, and we had to raise him, and that it was hard for me to obtain the food and cook it. Nothing helped. Then I would give way to tears. Alone. Almost always I was completely alone.

1914. War. What was going on in the city was dreadful. All the men were drafted. Panic set in. There wasn't a house free of suffering. My husband was deferred because of his illness. There was nowhere to earn a cent. I set myself to sewing sheepskin coats for the front. It was dirty and very heavy work. You needed a lot of lime, and from that I got an eye inflammation. I almost went blind. To drop this work would mean having no bread.

1915. Zaia came down with diphtheria. With great difficulty, through some kind of miracle, we managed to save him. In September our second child, Masha, appeared.[69] I was the only one working, supporting the family. My husband seldom had work. And his family, the freeloaders, did nothing and didn't want to do anything except take the last things we had. They were not embarrassed to walk in, rummage around the cupboard, and take whatever they liked. It was awkward to say anything while they were there, but when they left, I would tell my husband that people should never just walk in and take what they want without asking. I don't do that. But all I heard in response was an angry retort that nothing here was mine, that everything was his, and if I didn't like it, I could go wherever I pleased. I tried to tell him that they were behaving badly, but right in front of me he would tell them, "Pay no attention to her. This is not her house, it's yours, because it's mine. If she doesn't like it, she can leave."

---

69 Masha was born on September 11 (11 Tishri), 1915. See GABO, f. 585, op. 1, f. 3, l. 290. She died in St. Petersburg on April 25, 2001.

This made them very happy. If earlier they hated me, now I was in their way. After they left, I would cry, reproach him in my desperation, but I never heard a comforting word from him to me—to the contrary, nothing but insults that it would be inappropriate to write down. I never heard words like that in any decent household, never mind from a husband who had spent two years pleading with me to marry him. [And this is what I deserved] for raising two children and working without pause.

Seeing how he treated me, his family tried to get him to divorce me. Every day they would show up spouting some kind of dirt about me that they themselves had invented, and he would make a scene in their presence. I lost my head. Being only twenty-three years old and having lived such a short life, despite its many difficulties, I had never heard such words used about me from anyone.[70] I had hoped and expected that my life would improve after marriage, and to my horror all my hopes were destroyed and I had no way out. I was alone in the whole world, with two little ones in my arms. After every one of these frequent scenes, I would think over and analyze my conduct. Perhaps I was in the wrong? But after not finding any evidence of my guilt, I concluded that I was in the way. Because my every step was criticized. No matter what I did and no matter how I did it, it was always wrong. Everything I did led to mockery, reproaches, and insults. As though I were good for nothing.

Through observation, I became convinced that my husband was quieter when his family wasn't around. I hadn't heard a good word from him in a long time, but he was quieter. His screaming frightened the children. When Aunt Gesia learned of this, she came to me and said, "Get your things. You'll live with me. You weren't unneeded before, and you won't be now. You've had enough suffering here. It turns out that you were right when you didn't want to marry him because you were afraid of his family, and I persuaded you. And what kind of suffering do you have now? No clothes, no food, not a kind word." He was ashamed, and what did he say? "I didn't get married so that my wife would live with you." At this point he promised Auntie that his family would stop visiting him and he would start living with me on good terms. He in fact began behaving better toward me, and I breathed a sigh of relief. I tried to forget, and life became calmer, but there was an empty place in my heart. My woman's love was poisoned.

Having had such a hard life, I had hoped to find comfort in marriage, to forget what was bad, to be loved by someone, and I ended up deceived forever.

---

70 She was accused of talking to men on the street.

What could I hope for now? For beatings? It would be better to be physically beaten than to be insulted and spit on daily. It's impossible to describe this or write it. Only someone who has been in my place could understand.

Happy at least that things had quieted down, I tried to please my husband in every way. I remember that during our scenes I often asked him, "What did I do? Tell me what you want and what you like and I'll provide it, if only to please you." But he never answered logical questions. In my opinion, he understood things poorly, because his selfishness and need for power got in his way.

Time was passing. Because of the war, life became harder. Every day people received sad news from the front, news of a family member killed in action. There had been a great deception. There was a general in the tsar's army, Rennenkampf, a German, and he undermined Russia's strength, sold it to the enemy, with the help of the tsarina, also a German.[71] He led the whole active army and the reserves into a trap, onto a bridge that had been mined. The best of our forces perished, and he ran away.[72]

There was no food. We had to live, and we wanted to eat. When there's nothing to eat, your hunger is even greater. The war was in its third year. The Germans were winning. Nobody believed that a victory over the enemy would be possible. There were, as always in such situations, rumors that Jews had profited from the war and were helping the Germans. There were rumors that they had secretly collected gold and sent it to Germany—medicine, too. This set off a new wave of hatred among anti-Semites. Jews, choking down tears, wept over their loved ones, killed in the war, and now they had to endure these insults from Russians as well. Yes! People get used to it, but nonetheless, every time it calls forth anguish and grief.[73]

Thus my life passed in poverty, and sometimes in trouble. Little by little, my husband forgot his promise to my aunt. Once again he began visiting his family, and it all started again, only more quietly.

---

71 In the same way, people falsely accused Jews of spying.
72 Doba-Mera repeats rumors that were circulating at the time. She believes rumors that discredit Germans but not those that discredit Jews. Pavel-Georg Karlovich von Rennenkampf took command of the First Army of the Northwest Front during the East Prussian Operation. His actions in the Battle of Tannenberg (August 17–September 2, 1914), particularly his poor coordination with the Second Army, commanded by General Samsonov, ended in a Russian defeat that included thirty thousand killed and ninety-five thousand captured. No official accusations of treason were made against Rennenkampf. He was executed by the Bolsheviks in 1918 for his refusal to join the Red Army.
73 Doba-Mera's use of the present tense here is probably not accidental.

1917. The birth of our third child, Rakhil'.[74] Life became even harder. I was at the limits of my strength, maintaining us, and his family didn't want to do anything. We had no bread, but Ukraine had bread. His family moved there, Abram and Malka were there, and they lived decently.[75] When my husband's family arrived, they ruined them, since as before they didn't want to work. Seeing that Malka hadn't left anything for them, some of them found work. Motia and Gitta worked. Eidlia stayed with us. She loved me and didn't want to go away with them.

The mother in their family played no role whatsoever. She was a quiet, pious woman, worn down by a large family and by grief. In addition, there was no harmony within the family. Everyone considered it vital to grab something, and naturally the whole burden fell on the shoulders of the mother, who bent beneath its weight. When she objected to something the children were doing, she would get only insults from them.

In their absence our family life improved. His sister Eidlia, now deceased, gave me moral support. She, poor thing, also had a hard time. Her family disliked her because of her goodness. My husband's father had hated her most. Despite the way he treated her, she often took care of him during his illness, up to the last moment of his life, at a time when others didn't want to. But then the mother demanded that Eidlia live with them in Ukraine. She, poor thing, didn't want to go, and for this reason I didn't want to let her, but since her mother requested it, she went. It turned out that nobody wanted to work there, and that's why they summoned her. There was a typhus epidemic, and the whole family came down with it. She took care of everyone, but when they had all regained their health and she got sick, there was nobody to look after her, and they sent her to the hospital where another patient, delirious, beat her up, and she died. I mourned her like my own sister. At this point I understood this family of cannibals. What could I, a stranger, expect from them, when they didn't want to care for their own sister, despite the fact that she had saved them all from death?

1917. The February Revolution in Russia. The end of autocracy. No one expected it. To overthrow Nicholas II, uproot the Romanov dynasty without a fight? Without bloodshed? Nobody even dreamed such a thing could happen. But it did. Officers drove along the streets, shouting, "The tsar is gone! Long live freedom!" Even though the people wanted this, at that moment everybody

---

74 Rakhil' was born on August 3 (28 Av), 1917.
75 Doba-Mera's brother Abram married Meilakh's sister Malka.

seemed to be under a spell. They were afraid it was a provocation. The newspaper came out. I clearly remember the first words: "Bloody Nicholas, who brought the Russian land to complete ruin, has voluntarily abdicated the throne. Power has passed to the Provisional Government, with Kerensky at its head."[76]

There were demonstrations. Music. People kissed. They congratulated each other. In short, it was a happy time. But people needed food, and there wasn't any. The war sucked up everything, and in addition the government was stupid. The tsar was preoccupied with the tsaritsa, and the tsaritsa with Rasputin. That's how it happened. People began returning from the front. They were indignant about the past, but not satisfied with the present either. They said that this was not yet a revolution, which was still in the future, and other people would lead it. Big posters started appearing with the words "Peace, Bread, and Freedom." And in fact, people had had enough of war and hunger.

October 1917. Power passed to the Bolsheviks. Our city had a Soviet government. It was headed by the lawyer Korndorf, a very decent man. He governed well. Order was maintained. Suddenly, misfortune hit. They said that Germans were marching on Russia. There was a call for volunteers to fight them. But there was hardly anybody left [who could fight]. It was the fourth year of the war. There were only old men, adolescents, and war invalids. They took the adolescents. The city was surrounded. The adolescents stood up poorly against the well-trained German army. Everybody hid like mice. There were arrests, executions. Looting and fires. On top of old tears came new ones. The Germans set up their own system. They appointed a *varta* and a kommandant.[77] The Haidamaks were all Russians; only the kommandant's staff was German.[78] The Germans took whatever was left in the city and sent packages home.

The city had an underground Bolshevik organization. It was active. The Bolsheviks took up positions not far from the city on the road to Moscow, fifteen to twenty kilometers outside Klintsy. I remember that the commander of

---

76 In fact, the first chairman of the Provisional Government was Prince Georgii L'vov. Alexander Kerensky replaced him.
77 *Varta*: guard (Ukrainian).
78 In 1918 Klintsy became a part of the so-called Ukrainian Hetmanate, headed by Pavlo Skoropadsky and dependent on the German army. In December 1918 Skoropadsky was replaced by the Directorate, headed by Simon Petliura. Petliura's mounted Cossacks (but not Skoropadsky's) called themselves "Haidamaks" in memory of the Ukrainian rebels of the eighteenth century.

the varta was somebody by the name of Pages. I don't know what his nationality was. He was worse than a beast. People rarely left an encounter with him alive, and if they did, they didn't stay that way for long. After the Germans retreated, they discovered walls in his apartment riddled with bullet holes. Since there were quite a number of traitors, a group of Bolsheviks had been arrested. Among them were Lifshits, Riva Krasnovskaia, and some Russian workers. They were tortured severely. Pages liked that kind of fun. He carried out his interrogations upstairs, and the prison was downstairs. After the interrogation he liked to see the prisoner to the stairs and shoot him as he went down, justifying himself by saying that the person had been trying to escape. He did that on occasions when he had gotten no information from the prisoner.

Since the front—that is, the armistice line between the Germans and the Bolsheviks—was close, the underground organization was in contact with the frontline unit [of the Red Army—MB], which supplied them with everything they needed. The prisoners were subjected to unimaginable torture, especially Lifshits and Krasnovskaia. To stop the torture, Lifshits promised to show them where the guns and Bolshevik publications were stored. And so he took them through the streets, into the woods, and as they marched him, not one heart, not even a bandit's, could stay indifferent to this pitiful, half-crazed man, almost not a human being anymore, who sacrificed himself for the people. Despite the torture, Lifshits didn't name names and didn't betray anyone.[79]

Soon partisans tore into the city from all directions. Whoever interfered with them was quickly taken away.[80] Since the workers were not happy about the Germans and Haidamaks, they helped the partisans.

The head of the varta, Pages, wanted to execute the prisoners, but Headquarters had wasted a lot of effort and money on them, so they brought them to the Novozybkov Prison. There they remained until the Bolsheviks returned. Lifshits was not fated to live long under Soviet power. His health was broken by the torture, and he died very young. As for Krasnovskaia, she is still alive but gave up [party—MB] work because of mental issues, a consequence of prison and torture.

After the appearance—that is, the raid—of the partisans, life became even more tense. The streets became dangerous at night. The Germans burned the buildings where they had been carrying out some kind of secret work. They didn't allow the fires to be put out. Everyone looked out on the street through a

---

79 Doba-Mera here contradicts what she just said.
80 And apparently shot.

crack in their gates or entryways and trembled for their house and family. Night robberies and murders became frequent. There were rumors that the Germans were leaving and the Bolsheviks would soon arrive. Rich people began to evacuate, fearing they would have to pay indemnities. Caravans loaded with valuables and other things were constantly on the way to railway stations. Our quiet little station came to life. It was packed with people and baggage. A din could be heard day and night. Trains with people and things were departing all the time, but it was beyond the ability of the railroad to move everybody out quickly.

The Black Hundreds started a rumor in the city that the Bolsheviks would start killing Jews first, since they were always the victims of disorder. The Jewish poor reacted to this provocation by leaving, and without anything to live on they left home and hearth and took off in unknown directions. This happened in December, and the winter was cold, so many people suffered harshly for their recklessness. I remember how we nervously stood at the gates and watched the endless wagons of people of different types making their escape. Our neighbor, a jeweler by the name of Reznikov, came up to us and asked what were we going to do, wait for our deaths here? At this time our relative, the doctor E. D. Poliakov, was passing by. Seeing our confusion, he asked, "What are you doing staring at crazy people who are running away from the Bolsheviks? Do you envy them—is that it? Listen! Rich people are leaving because they fear for their capital. But why would a poor person leave? They fall victim to rumors and then pay for it harshly. The Red Army is coming, commanded by Shchors, and it won't hurt anyone except Haidamaks who are trying to hide.[81] Whoever disobeys the orders and mistreats the civilian population will be tried in a military court." Then we calmed down and went back into the house. Only the children were crying, trembling with fear.

During the partisan raid on the city, a boy of around ten was caught in the crossfire and wounded. At that time we were living in Isaev's house. In the courtyard was a big root cellar, and when the shooting began, I grabbed the children and went there, since we would not be in danger from the bullets there. Seeing a little boy covered in blood, I took him too, and since I always had iodine and bandages with me, I wrapped the wound on his arm. When things calmed down, he was sent to the hospital. To this day I don't know who this boy was.

---

81 In October and November the Red Army under the command of Shchors fought the Germans and the Hetmanates; in December they fought the Cossacks of the Directorate.

We had a little cow. And as soon as people started to say that there would be fighting, Papa [Doba-Mera's husband] would take the cow to Grandmother's [his mother's—MB]. We lived in the center of town, and Grandmother lived on the outskirts; he also thought it was safer there. We had a neighbor named Panizovskii. As soon as he heard rumors about fighting, he would calm everyone with a quip, "Since Medvedev hasn't taken his cow to his mother's, there's no cause for alarm."

I remember that the Germans set fire to the warehouse across from us. It was like daylight, and it was terrible. Nobody was in charge of the city. They didn't allow the fire to be put out, and you couldn't go out on the street.[82] People stood in their courtyards and trembled with fear that the fire would spread to the houses. Fortunately, this didn't happen. In the morning, the city was empty. People were afraid to stick their noses out of their houses. Gradually they emerged and decided to organize a patrol to protect the city from irresponsible elements [robbers?—MB]. My husband joined because he liked things like that, plus it was really necessary. They guarded the city, patrolling like soldiers with guns on their shoulders, until the Bolsheviks came. Everything was under control. Then one night a drunk came walking along. They shouted "Halt," but it didn't even occur to him to stop. Then the guard had to shoot. He shot in the air three times, but the drunk didn't stop. Then he had to actually shoot him, but because he didn't want to kill him, he shot him in the leg.

There were no other incidents. People were fed up with living under the Germans, and they couldn't wait for the Bolsheviks to come. I remember that they entered the city on December 18, 1918. Since we lived in the center, all the events took place around us. They were met with bread and salt. Before the army entered, a reconnaissance group came on horseback to see if there were any enemies in hiding. They talked with the residents. After them came the army with Shchors at its head. While they were being billeted in various places, despite the severe frost they filled the streets. There was a huge rally across from our house. Since the army needed to be fed, people were asked to help the front and bake bread from army flour. Some people responded, including us. My husband and I volunteered to bake bread for them. Shchors himself came to see us, and he liked us a lot, and our bread was the best. As long as the army was in our city, he came to see us often and joked with our children. We liked him a lot. He had a very kind face. He wore a short leather jacket, with a holster on his hip.

---

82 This incident was described earlier.

It's interesting that during the German occupation a lame, bearded beggar would often stand by our house. I often brought him something to eat. A couple of days after the Bolsheviks came, he reappeared young and healthy, without his crutches, and greeted me with the question, "Do you recognize me?" How could I recognize him? Then he told me that his mission had been to observe things and especially the actions of the Haidamaks. Since most of them spent their time getting drunk in the club, and the club was across the street from us, that's where he stood. He also spied on traitors from the population and, risking his life, reported this information to Headquarters. He thanked us for supporting him and gave the children sugar. And this meeting was so wonderful that we will never forget it. Where is this hero now? How stupid of us that we never found out his last name or where he was from. It happens that you don't think of things in time, and then you regret it but there is no going back.

The army left for the front, and the city was turned over to the civilian Soviet authority headed by the Cheka.[83] At first people were fearful. As always, especially in the provinces, people who knew each other and were often at odds went to the Cheka and informed on those they disliked: this one, they said, is a Haidamak, and that one is a traitor. But the Cheka figured things out quickly and would say to the informant, "if your accusations turn out to be false, then the punishment meant for the guilty party will be yours." And people started to inform on each other less frequently. Little by little, life began to take shape. But the Civil War heated up in the city, and once again the bourgeoisie raised its head.

[p. 215. End of the first notebook.]

Second Notebook [1937]

[Begins on p. 258. The earlier pages describing two decades of life were destroyed.—MB]

At this point I became convinced that our life had just entered a period of calm, but that the slightest disturbance would make it erupt like a volcano. That period of calm was because there were no causes or instigators, but if there were any, the troubles would come back at us with great severity. [The underlined words were crossed out.—MB]

---

83 The Cheka or VChK, the All-Russian Extraordinary Commission for the Struggle against Counterrevolution and Sabotage, was the Bolshevik political police, the precursor of the KGB.

I continued to feel ill. The year was 1937. We were again in Leningrad, in Perekupnoi Lane. We had managed to get rid of the other family, but we had only one room with light coming in, and that greatly affected my health.[84] We always had a light on. It was very difficult for me to look after the family, and aside from Rakhil', nobody wanted to help. We did put food on the table, but barely. There was, of course, no money for clothes. Then we moved to Mytninskaia. We were lured there by much better rooms. But the other woman living there was a poisoned candy. Before we got there, she had managed to get rid of the previous family that lived there, and they were Russian, so we had it even worse. The apartment was torture. There were additional heart attacks. In the morning everyone would leave, and I alone would try to put all the pieces together. Time passed. The children were growing. Gessel' was finishing technical school,[85] as was Rakhil'. He was drafted. Zaia and Masha left home—they were the ones we had hoped would help the younger children get started.

The war was unexpected.[86] Like all tragedies it came without warning. Right before that, Rakhil' had met Sasha.[87] Everybody was sent to the front—Sasha, Rakhil', and Ges'ka. Despite the boasting that we would rout the Finns, it turned out the other way. They were experienced soldiers. With good provisions and light, warm clothing. Our boys didn't even have felt boots. There were heavy frosts. Our soldiers froze. If and when they did get warm clothing, the officers were given white coats, and the soldiers got yellow ones. Finnish snipers had no trouble finding the officers. In addition, our uniforms were heavy, and our soldiers could hardly turn around in their sheepskin coats, while the Finns had worsted and wool. By the time we adapted to their methods, the advantage was already on their side.

The war was a tremendous blow to my poor health, and in addition I was in some kind of stupor. One night Gessel' arrived from the front, nearly frozen. In light boots and a greatcoat, in the severe cold. He didn't want

---

84 After the October Revolution, individual apartments in large cities were required to take on additional tenants. This was the beginning of communal apartments, in which several unrelated families lived together, sharing a single kitchen, toilet, and bath (assuming there was one).

85 Gessel' (Gesel' according to his birth certificate), the fourth child, was born in Klintsy on December 21, 1918. He died in the United States around 1988.

86 The Russo-Finnish War of 1939–1940. See Michael Beizer's introduction.

87 Sasha (Sulia or Srul') Moshkovich (1911–1974) was Michael Beizer's father. He was born in the village of Bronniki, Zaslavskii District, Volyn' Province. After serving in the army, he did not return to the village but settled in Leningrad. He was wounded in World War II and lived as a disabled veteran. He died in Leningrad.

anything—not to eat, not to drink—only to get warm. We warmed him with hot water bottles, with irons, and we barely succeeded. He asked us to get him up the next morning at eleven. We covered him with my soft squirrel-fur coat, and he fell asleep. In the morning everyone left; I was alone. I awakened him on time. My heart broke. He jumped up, frightened, threw off my coat, and shouted, "Why did you give me a wounded man's blanket? I'm not wounded." I comforted him, I said that he was home, and it wasn't a blanket, it was my coat. He calmed down a little. "Mamochka, forgive me," he said, "I frightened you." He turned down the food I offered him and ran off. I ran after him. I watched him run down the stairs. My tears flowed, but I stood there in a stupor. His tracks disappeared. I returned to consciousness, closed the door, and went inside, but being unable to find a place for myself, I went out again.

There another surprise awaited me. A policeman started harassing me, saying that I was following him, and wanted to take me to the station. This only made things worse. Frightened, I barely made it home and for a long time couldn't get back to normal. Finally I managed to calm down and do some housework.

It was 1940. The terrible war with the Finns, which had caused many deaths, was over. Rakhil′ and Sasha came back from the front. They got married. They moved in with us. Once again my stomach acted up, and I was put in the hospital. How much money was spent on my recovery! They issued me a death sentence. Papa went on vacation to a sanatorium. Despite my serious condition, I was left alone. Everyone was working. Ida alone kept house for everyone. Would a woman leave her bedridden husband and go on vacation? But that's what he did. He wasn't young anymore. Perhaps he wanted a freer life.

Masha and Kolia graduated.[88] We had long since made peace with them. Their student years had been difficult. They were very poor, and we couldn't help them. Two grandchildren appeared: Ed and Vova.[89] We hadn't experienced much joy in life and here we were already a grandfather and grandmother. After graduating, Masha and Kolia were sent away to Borisoglebsk to

---

88 Nikolai (Kolia) Sergeevich Berezovskii (1911, Katel′nichi–1988, Leningrad). Masha and Kolia were in the same class at the Leningrad Refrigeration Institute and married when Masha was nineteen.
89 Eduard (Ed) Izrail′evich Medvedev (1937–2008) was Zaia's oldest son. Vladimir (Vova) Nikolaevich Berezovskii (1938–2007) was Masha and Kolia's only son. A graduate of Leningrad University, he worked as a geologist. He died in April 2007, right after returning from a trip to Israel.

work.[90] When I got out of the hospital, feeling somewhat better, I took Ida and set off for Borisoglebsk for the summer at Masha's request.

The memorable year 1941. As we were leaving Leningrad, we heard that the Germans had deployed twelve divisions against us in Finland.[91] Sensing disaster, Auntie Gesia [by then Gesia Belkina lived in Leningrad—MB], who was seeing us off, was distressed because she felt we might never see one another again. Despite our anxiety, I didn't pack anything warm. We arrived in Borisoglebsk at the end of May. Masha was living in a good apartment. Materially she was not doing badly. Vova went to nursery school. I would pick him up there and look after him myself. Masha didn't do any cooking because she had no time. This resulted in a lot of expense, so I myself started cooking, which improved their situation a lot. As the international situation grew more tense, Masha and Kolia were sent to Khar´kov to get military training.

Suddenly it was war! My God! I was overcome with terror. My children, my children would have to face fire. I was away. Masha was gone. How would they manage at home without me? My mind was racing in all directions, but I couldn't find any solution. Go to Leningrad? But what about Vova? Take him with me? But then what would Masha do? How would we find each other in the midst of fire? The terror of this dead end is indescribable.

I got a telegram from Papa in Leningrad telling us not to come, because there would be no way of getting there. In my opinion, this was the one intelligent decision of his entire life. Masha also sent a telegram saying that they would return soon. The radio broadcasts from the Informburo were terrifying. The war was proceeding with lightning speed. Everything, everywhere, was on fire. Grandmother sent a final letter, saying that she did not know what to do.[92] Apparently she wanted to come to live with me. I sent her a telegram telling her to come immediately, and that we were not in danger. But either she didn't get it or she could no longer leave. From my stepsister Meita I got a final letter saying that Novozybkov was burning and she didn't know how to save herself.

---

90 In the Soviet Union university graduates were assigned to work at industries and institutes, in many cases very far from their homes. They did not have the right to choose where they went. In addition, beginning in 1940 it was forbidden to change jobs on one's own initiative, and criminal penalties were instituted for skipping work or coming late. Borisoglebsk is a city in Voronezh District, more than a thousand kilometers from Leningrad.
91 These rumors proved correct.
92 Meilakh's mother, Khaia-Reize, was killed during the German occupation of Klintsy.

The children were at the front. Gessel´ left with the first callup. Isaak volunteered from school.[93] My son-in-law Sasha was at the Leningrad front. Leningrad was being bombed. There was no food. The blockade began. Masha came. Refugees filled the railway stations, the streets, the homes of peasants.[94] Hungry people in rags, without roof or food, wandered everywhere, and little attention was paid to them. I looked intently at everyone, trying to identify acquaintances and help those unfortunates if I found them. I recognized people from my faraway Khotimsk. Despite my unhappy life in my birthplace, it was still pleasant for me to remember it. Because childhood amusements and pleasures remain in your memory your whole life long. I was happy to see these people. They were the two Userov sisters, Khaia and Masha. Masha had a husband and a child. They looked terrible. They lived in a peasant's house and slept on the bare, dirty floor. They didn't have time to take anything from home, as they were running from the bombing and could no longer return because the city was already burning. That was Mogilev. Without thinking, I gave them my address. Kolia helped me, and I helped them as best I could. Because Papa had taught me: "The rich are happy. They will get along without you. You help where there is sorrow." And so all my life I helped those in need, not thinking about whether they would be grateful or not. At times like that you don't think.

Reports from Leningrad made it clear that people had to evacuate. I sent expedited telegrams to Papa, telling him to leave. He was working as a transportation supervisor. He could have brought all his things with him. We could have sold everything and survived. But Papa had other ideas. He got almost all his workers out, together with their junk, including their old iron bedsteads, and didn't give a thought to himself. Masha asked me: "Why are you holding Papa back? Leningrad is burning." I was offended. She had forgotten how stubborn he was. The world could turn inside out, and he would do what he wanted. Rakhil´ and the baby didn't listen to him and left. He didn't give her things to take, convinced that the Germans would fall into a trap and that would be the end of them. Then I wrote him a letter that said the following: "Masha doesn't

---

93 Isaak (Isia) Medvedev (1922–1979) was the fifth child of Doba-Mera and Meilakh. He was a tank officer at the front. He married Zoia, a nurse, who was Russian.

94 According to the "politically correct" terminology of that period, all civilians who left their hometowns to travel east, either by train or on foot, were called evacuees. But many of them were simply refugees, who evacuated on their own. The percentage of Jews among evacuees was significantly higher than in the population at large. See Rebecca Manley, *To the Tashkent Station: Evacuation and Survival in the Soviet Union at War* (Ithaca, NY: Cornell University Press, 2009), 114.

believe that I am insisting that you join us. I ask you to come immediately, while it is still possible." I gave this to Masha to read. She read it and says, "You'll see, now he'll come." The answer came that he had no intention of leaving. Masha and Kolia were distressed. "How did you set things up so that Papa doesn't listen to you?" Well, youth is stupid. But now, at such a time! The children had already turned into adults, and Papa remained the same. He had a saying: "What I want, that's what I'll do." Because of this stubbornness of his, he nearly destroyed not only himself but also Zaia, who had stayed behind to look after him.

Rakhil' wound up in Kotel'nichi, with Kolia's parents. Because the bigs shots were evacuating, and they didn't want to go to the boondocks, far from Moscow (they were looking for apartments in Borisoglebsk). One of those people had his eye on Kolia's apartment and his job, so quite unexpectedly Kolia got transferred to Orsk. I was in horror. How could they travel at such a terrible time? Among the evacuees were people who lost children and other family members. Almost everyone was seized with sadness and terror. We (Ida and I) didn't want to travel with Masha at a time like that, so as not to be a burden to them. But Kolia and Masha didn't want to abandon us, and we went together. Masha comforted us saying that it was for the best, because we didn't know what would happen to Borisoglebsk. My heart was torn into pieces. Papa was in blockaded, starving Leningrad. Zaia was with him because he didn't want to abandon Papa, so he didn't leave. Gessel', Isaak, and Sasha were at the front. So was Abram's Misha.[95] I stopped sleeping. Tears didn't dry in my eyes. That was only the beginning—how much more grief would the war bring? The war was expanding. Grief mounted. People had already received notifications of the deaths of their relatives at the front.

Our journey began. Since Borisoglebsk was not a railway hub, we had to travel several hours and then change at Povorino. When we got to the Povorino station, it was chaos. Refugees from Ukraine and Bessarabia. People of different nationalities. The majority were Jews. The station was packed with people. Some were just leaving home, and others were running

---

95 Abram and Malka Gurevich had moved to the Jewish kolkhoz (collective farm) *Naye lebn* (New Life [Yiddish]) in Crimea. They had two sons and a daughter: Moisei (Mikhail; 1919–1945), Izrail' (1926–1944), and Rakhil' (1922–1979). Both sons were killed at the front at the end of the war. Mikhail Gurevich, who had become a divisional reconnaissance commander, was killed by a German sniper on February 3, 1945, in Czechoslovakia (from a letter of the Red Army soldier Petia, a wartime friend of M. A. Gurevich, to Gurevich's girlfriend in the rear, February 5, 1945. Archive of Michael Beizer).

as though from a fire—tormented, in rags. Everyone was in a bad mood. Strong people tried to push away the weak, which was easy to accomplish. When the train was arriving, nobody knew. Could it accommodate everyone?—nobody knew that either. For us, just leaving home, it was terrible to see what was happening. Hearing about how children got lost [and knowing—MB] that our Vova couldn't stay long in one place, I hung a locket on his neck; inside the locket was a piece of paper with his name on it and who to tell in case he got lost. When he saw this terrible scene, Kolia got upset, found himself a corner, and fell asleep.

Suddenly the train came. Over our heads flew things, people, children. There was screaming and crying, and no Kolia. Go find a sleeping man in a pile of so many other sleeping men. And the train was already crammed with people; it had come from Ukraine. Finally we found Kolia. Frightened, he came running. We began to drag our things. And now profiteers started to load their things, and we, inexperienced idiots, instead of taking our places, stood there and let them move their things through, and they assured us that they were just finishing. When they had loaded everything, it turned out that the whole compartment was filled with their things, and there was no room for us or our things, so we stood at the end of the vestibule by the toilet and the door. In that position we traveled several days and nights. At last we reached the city of Molotov [Perm'—MB], where some people got off, and we got one seat for all of us. At least we could sit Vova down. Most of the people were like beasts. They took the upper and the lower bunks, and sick people and children sat on the floor or stood by the door. There were families of means who had arranged with the conductor to set themselves up in his compartment. When the train came to a halt, people ran out for water. A lot of them were women. The men pushed them away, and fights started. I can't describe the horror that surrounded us, the whole nightmare of our trip to Kuibyshev [Samara—MB]. Before we got there, we ran into Adol'f Gusakov.[96] He was traveling farther, but we got off.

Kuibyshev was on edge.[97] It was under blackout. The train station was packed with people. Tickets weren't being punched; people weren't allowed onto trains.[98] We got into one train through the window, but somebody told

---

96 The husband of Meilakh's sister Sima.
97 The Soviet government had escaped from Moscow to Kuibyshev in October 1941.
98 That is, despite the fact that the ticket had been purchased, they were not given their assigned seat. The ticket with its seat, car, and train assignments had not been punched through, making it illegal for them to be on the train.

the conductor, and he made us leave. Vova and I were sent to the resting area. I had barely fallen asleep when Vova ran off, undressed. Where he ran, he himself didn't know, but luckily Masha, Kolia, and Ida were standing across from the staircase he ran down. They saw him in the mirror and grabbed him without thinking, a stroke of luck that saved us our health. Where would we have even looked for him, the silly child? Finally we left, without ever having our tickets punched. In the train, already moving, we had to pay a fine. The ride was hideous. The train moved only at night. The cars looked like they were the very first ever to be built. You often heard anti-Semitic slurs, which used to be rare. We got to Chkalov [Orenburg—MB] half-alive. We needed to get to Orsk to change trains, and our train was going to Tashkent. We had to wait for the Orsk train. Vova was put in the children's room, from which he ran away. They found him because of the note, but the locket with its chain had been stolen by the staff there. Here Kolia was able to negotiate a cabin for us. After a long and difficult journey, we were seated in a cabin, and it was hard to believe that we had come out of the whole thing alive, after so many tribulations, without sleep, and without rest. Ida had it worst of all, because she ended up in the vestibule full of baggage, where she couldn't walk through or even move from her spot or sit down. She stood like that for over two days and two nights.

At last we reached Orsk. A car was sent to pick us up, and we arrived at a building where we were given two rooms, one about twenty square meters and the other about eight. After all we had been through, it seemed like paradise. We were surprised when the administrator asked us what kind of furniture to bring in. It turned out later that he [judging from the way we looked—MB] had decided that we had never slept in a bed. But this didn't concern me. Other thoughts gave me no peace. Where is my family? Almost everyone was under fire. Beginning with Papa and his stubbornness, because of which Zaia was suffering. Gessel' and Isaak were at the front. And Sasha was there, and Abram's Misha too. There was no news from anyone. Then we started hearing the "good" news that in places under German occupation the Jews had all been annihilated.[99] That meant we had lost Grandmother and all our Novozybkov relatives. In sum, "joy" filled our hearts. Rakhil' and Tema were in Kotel'nichi, with Kolia's parents.[100] There were no letters from Leningrad. Where my Abram was, I also had no idea.

---

99 We see that at the end of 1941 Doba-Mera already knew about this.
100 Michael Beizer's older sister Tema Slobodinskaia (Beizer) was born on March 13, 1941. Since 1991 she has been living in Jerusalem.

But life makes its demands. I became the cook and the nanny, and Kolia and Masha worked. Ida went to school, but she helped me. Winter came. Ida and I had neither clothes nor shoes. One time Kolia asked me, "What do you think about Rakhil´?" "What should I think?" I answered, "We ourselves aren't independent." I meant that we were hanging on his neck—how could I go and send for Rakhil´ too? If Papa had been with us, it would have been another story. Kolia didn't bring this up with me again. Some time passed, and a wagon drove up to our door. Kolia got off, carrying a baby, and after him came an old woman I didn't know. They came inside, and the woman threw herself into my arms with a wild, heartrending shriek, "Mamochka! Now I'm saved, because I am with you." It turned out that after our conversation, Kolia sent her an official invitation, because without this invitation you couldn't get train tickets. He didn't say a word to us. That's how nobly he behaved to us, despite the fact that we hadn't been happy about his marriage to Masha, and he knew that.

The war was raging in earnest. There were no letters from any of the children or from Papa. We lived with Masha. Rakhil´ worked. Ida went to school. I looked after everyone. I took care of two children: Vova, who was small, and Tema, who was tiny. Vova would beat up Tema, and sometimes she fell down because nobody was watching her. Ida helped me as best she could, but she was the only one. From the absence of letters and the heavy work at home, I often got sick. But then we got a letter from Ges´ka, sent to other people. They brought it to us. He asked if they knew whether anyone from his family was still alive. He himself was severely wounded, recuperating in Buzuluk in the Urals. You can imagine how many tears I shed and how I tried to go see him, but they weren't issuing tickets. Then I tried to get him moved to the hospital in Orsk, but I wasn't successful in that either.

December 1941. Kolia was taken into the army, meaning he joined the war. The family now consisted of women and children. All our men were at the front, and now we were losing him, our sole support. He had a release from the draft, but his director disliked him and wanted him out. Friends who understood our situation got him a temporary deferment. This was December 31, 1941. When at eleven o'clock he returned from military headquarters, our joy knew no bounds. Papa and Zaia were in blockaded Leningrad. Where Isia and Sasha were, nobody knew. Misha, our nephew, sent occasional letters. From places under German occupation came terrible news. They said that all the Jews had been annihilated. More grief. Grandmother, my sisters, my sister Meita, and the other relatives, and in general everybody was a blood relation.[101] My heart broke into pieces, but it was impossible to change anything. In the daytime I ran like a squirrel on a wheel; at night, tears.

At last a letter came from Abram. It turned out that he had passed through Orsk but did not stop to see us; he didn't want to disturb us. Idiocy on his part. At that time complete strangers stayed with us and thought nothing of it. Finally came the joyful news that the siege of Leningrad was broken. How many lives that cost. Papa and Zaia came from Leningrad. Both in frightening condition.[102] Zaia was tolerable, but Papa was swollen. I looked at him and said, "What kind of famine could there have been in Leningrad if Papa looks like this!" I didn't understand immediately that he was half-dead.

End of the second notebook.

---

101 During the Nazi occupation of Klintsy, more than three thousand Jews were killed. A decree of the city commission from April 5, 1944, following the liberation of Klintsy, gives wrenching details of the mass shooting in December 1941. One of the local residents who had been forced to bury the dead, said, "My hands trembled. A mother clutched a happy little child to her breast, but the bullet missed and the child remained alive. I covered him with earth, and he pushed it away with his little hands and giggled. It grew dark before my eyes. I left the pit, stumbled, and fell." See State Archive of the Russian Federation (GARF), f. 7021, op. 19, d. 5, l. 9.

102 Some 750,000–800,000 people died from hunger and shelling during the siege of Leningrad.

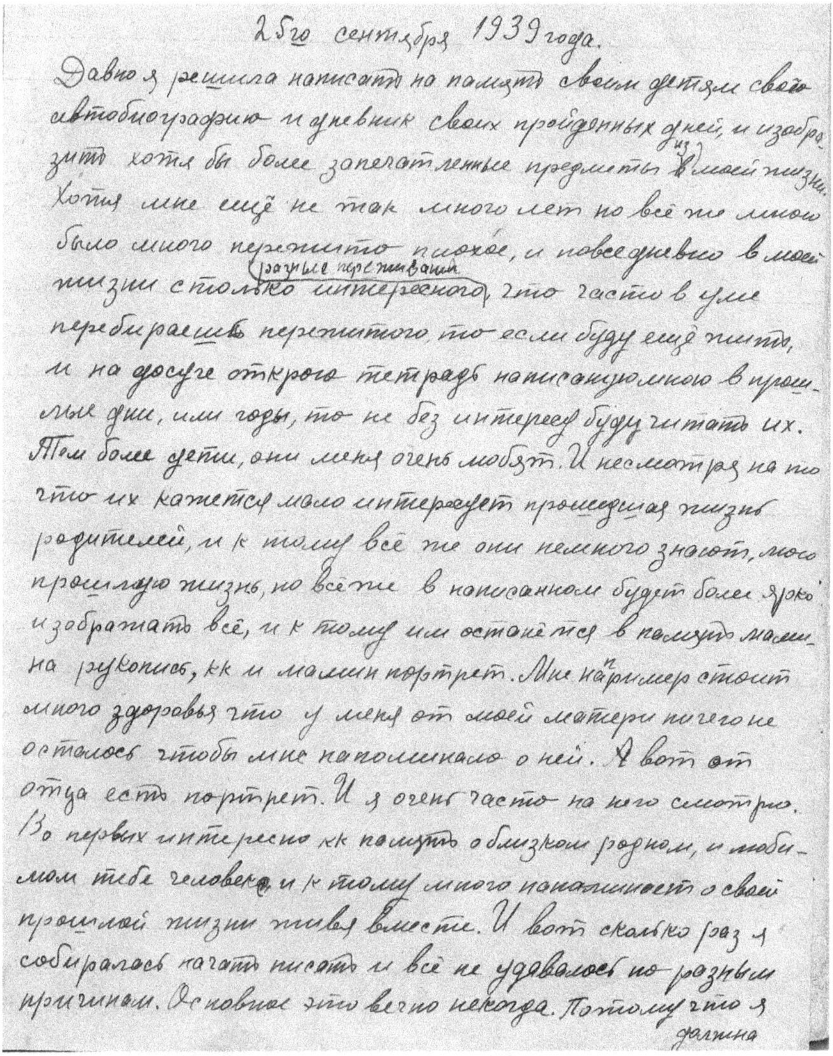
25го сентября 1939 года.
Давно я решила написать на память своим детям свою
автобиографию и дневник своих пройденных дней, и изобра-
зить хотя бы более запечатленные предметы (из) в моей жизни.
Хотя мне ещё не так много лет но всё же много
было много пережито плохое, и повседневно в моей
жизни столько (разные переживания) интересного, что часто в уме
перебираешь пережитого, то если буду ещё жить,
и на досуге открою тетрадь написанную мною в прош-
лые дни, или годы, то не без интереса буду читать их.
Тем более дети, они меня очень любят. И несмотря на то
что их кажется мало интересует прошедшая жизнь
родителей, и к тому всё же они немного знают, мою
прошлую жизнь, но всё же в написанном будет более ярко
изображать всё, и к тому им останется в память мами-
на рукопись, кк и мамин портрет. Мне например стоит
много здоровья что у меня от моей матери ничего не
осталось чтобы мне напоминало о ней. А вот от
отца есть портрет. И я очень часто на него смотрю.
Во первых интересно кк память о близком родном, и люби-
мом тебе человеке и к тому много напоминает о своей
прошлой жизни живя вместе. И вот сколько раз я
собиралась начать писать и всё не удавалось по разным
причинам. Основное это вечно некогда. Потому что я
должна

Fig. 11 The opening page of Doba-Mera's memoir.

Index

A
Alexander II, 31n3, 96n56
Alter (Doba-Mera's uncle), 13, 15, 43–49, 86, 112, 115, 119, 121–123
America, 9, 75, 108–109
Andrzhevskii, 92
anti-Semitism, 5, 9, 64–65, 71, 76, 85, 129, 142
Azava, Natasha, vi
Azriel' (Doba-Mera's cousin, son of Rokha and Izrail'), 58

B
Beizer (née Medvedeva), Rokhlya-Lea (Doba-Mera's daughter), 4, 25–26, 130, 136–137, 139–140, 142–143
Beizer, Roza, 27
Beizer, Sasha (Sulia; Doba-Mera's son-in-law), 4–5, 26, 136–137, 139–140, 142–143
Belkina, Gesia (Doba-Mera's aunt), 3, 12–14, 17–18, 43, 46, 48, 54–55, 59, 92, 94, 112, 116–118, 125, 128, 138
Berezovskaia (née Medvedeva), Maria (Masha; Doba-Mera's daughter), 25–26, 127, 136–143
Berezovskii, Nikolai (Kolia), 137–143
Berezovskii, Vladimir (Vova) 27, 137, 138, 141, 142–143
Black Hundreds, 21, 64–65, 67, 69–70, 133
Bolsheviks, 20–21, 61n32, 131–135
Borisoglebsk, 137–140
Briansk, vi, 77, 91
Brodskii Hospital, 13, 97
Brushtein, Fania, 38n11, 49

C
Chechersk, 34
Cheremkhovo, 5
Chernigov Province, vi, 2, 3n7, 31n3
Cohen, Jocelyn, 10
Communist Party, 4, 6, 64–65
Cossacks, 19, 62n34, 63–64, 73, 131n78, 133n81
Crimea, 120, 140n95

D
Der Fraynd, 30
distillation business, 70, 72
Dolgov, Petr Petrovich, 57, 69
Donskaia rech' (publishing house), 80
Dymentman, Anna, vi

E
Eakin, Paul John, 7–8
Ekaterinoslavl', 95
"enemies of the people," 5

F
Freeze, ChaeRan, vi

G
Gomel', 43, 83–84, 103, 124
Gordin, Jacob, *see Khasye di yesoyme*
Gurevich (Medvedev), Izrail'-Vel'ka (Doba-Mera's father), 1, 11–18, 20, 23, 29, 31–55, 57–59, 70, 73, 76, 78, 82–83, 86, 89–90, 92, 94–106, 108, 112–113, 116, 118, 123
Gurevich, Avrom-Yudl (Abram; Doba-Mera's brother), 3, 12, 34–36, 41–42, 51, 53, 57–59, 102–106, 116, 130, 140–144
Gurevich, Malka

H
Ha-Melits, 30
Ha-Ne'ehavim veha-ne'imim; oder, Der shvartser yingermantshik (The Beloved and the

Pleasant, or the Black Young Man) by Jacob Dineson [Yankev Dinezon], 45
Haidamaks, 131–133, 135

I
Ilovaiskii, Dmitrii, 17, 52
Itskov, Mendel, 78

J
Jewish cantonists, 96
Jewish Enlightenment, 1, 39n12
Jewish self-defense, 20, 71–75, 77

K
Kerensky, Alexander, 131
Khasye di yesoyme (Khasia the orphan), 119
Khazanov, Aleksandr Mendelevich, 40n13
Khazanov, Leib, 39, 40n13, 69n39
Khazanov, Mendel, 5
Khazanova, Liubov' (Liuba), 1, 69n39
Khokhmes Shloyme (The Wisdom of Solomon), 33
Khotimsk (shtetl), 1, 5, 11, 19, 29, 40n13, 43–44, 53–54, 59n31, 71n42, 72n44, 73, 78, 83, 86, 93, 95–96, 102–103, 105, 112, 118–119, 121–123, 139
Khrushchev, Nikita, 5
Kiev, 13–14, 96–100, 121, 126
Kirov, Sergei M., 4n15
Kishinev pogrom, 75n47
Klimovichi District, 1, 73, 79, 120
Klintsy, 3–4, 23–24, 26, 41, 48, 53–55, 59–61, 65–66, 69–70, 74, 77, 92–93, 95–96, 103, 105, 111–113, 116n62, 118–119, 121, 123, 131, 136n85, 138n92, 144n101
Kosiukovich (nearest railway station to Khotimsk), 1
Krasnopol', 58
Krasnovskaia, Riva, 61–62, 132
Kunstkamera, St. Petersburg, vi

L
Leningrad Choral Synagogue, 6
Leningrad, 4–6, 22, 25, 27, 124, 136, 138–140, 142–144. *See also* St. Petersburg
Levashovo, 5–7, 28
Liova (radical who shares literature with Doba-Mera in 1905), 20, 53, 79–81
lishenets, 3–4
Lyfsha (Doba-Mera's aunt), 16, 42–44, 46–49, 59, 112, 119–120

M
Marx, Karl, 20, 81
Marxism, 9, 14–16, 20
May 1, 16, 84
Medvedev, Ben'iamin, 2
Medvedev, Berka (Borukh), 2–3
Medvedev, David, 3, 12, 35, 68
Medvedev, Ed (Eduard), 27, 137
Medvedev, Gessel' (Ges'ka; Doba-Mera's son), 136, 139–140, 142–143
Medvedev, Girsh, 114–115
Medvedev, Isaak, 25, 139–140, 142
Medvedev, Izrail' (Doba-Mera's uncle), 41, 53, 55–56, 58, 78, 93, 117
Medvedev, Izrail' (Zaia)-Vel'ka (Doba-Mera's son), 25–26, 124–127, 136, 137n89, 140, 142–144
Medvedev, Khayim Yankel, 2
Medvedev, Meilakh (Doba-Mera's husband), 2–6, 22, 24–27, 108–115, 119–130, 134, 137–144
Medvedev, Veniamin (Venia), vi, 6–7, 53n28
Medvedev, Vova, 27
Medvedev, Yankel-Moyshe (Iakov-Meisha) Berkovich, 3, 104, 108, 116n62, 121–123, 125, 130
Medvedev, Yankel-Moyshe (Iakov-Meisha) Berkovich, 3, 104, 108, 116n62, 121–123, 125, 130
Medvedeva, Freida, 92–93
Medvedeva, Ida (Eidlia), vi, 7, 25, 27, 137–138, 140, 142–143
Medvedeva, Khana (wife of Girsh), 115
Medvedeva, Rivka, 2
Medvedeva, Rokhl'-Leah (Doba-Mera's mother), 1–2, 4, 12, 17, 25, 29, 33–38, 40–44, 46–54, 57–58, 87, 91–93, 102–103, 108, 116–117
Medvedeva, Roza, 27
Medvedeva, Zina, 27
Mkhiras Yoysef (The Sale of Joseph), 33
Mogilev Province, 1, 29, 31n3, 80
Mogilev, 139
Moz, Michael, vi

N
Nakhimovsky, Alexander, vi
New Economic Policy (NEP), 1922–1928, 3, 4n12
Newman, Roberta, vi, 74n46
Nicholas I, 96

Nicholas II, 36, 61–62, 86, 130–131
Novozybkov Prison, 132
Novozybkov, 59, 138, 142
numerus clausus, 30n2

O
Obolenskii, Prince, 71n42, 72
Old Believers, 3n7, 62, 66
Orel Province, 80, 88
Orsha pogrom, 75
Orsk, 5, 140, 142–144

P
Pages, 132
Pale of Settlement, 8, 9, 11, 30n2, 61n33, 76, 88, 96, 101
Pargolovo, 6
Pishchik, Khacha, 77
pogroms, 2, 9–11, 18, 20, 61n33, 66–75, 90
Poliakov, Motia, 107
Pushkin, Alexander, 40

R
rabfak, 4
Red Army, 21, 132–133
Riabinkii, Aizik, 82–83
Rogachev pogrom, 75
Rogachev, 75, 94
Rokha (Doba-Mera's aunt, wife of Izrail'), 58
Roslavl', 76, 78, 81
Rubinchik, Fania, 16, 38
Russian Revolution (1905–1907), 2, 19, 61n33
Russian Revolution (1917), 4, 40, 130–131, 136n84

S
Shandler, Jeffrey, 9–10
Shchors, Nikolai Aleksandrovich, General, 4, 21, 133–134
Shifrin, 20
Shifrin, Evgenii, 1
Shifrin, Shevel', 71n42, 73–74, 80
Shklov pogrom, 75
Sholem Aleichem, 13, 44, 76
Sholokhova, Lyudmila, vi, 74n46
Shrayer, Maxim D., vi

shtreykbrekher, 20, 62
Shumiachi, 58
Sirkis, Yoel (a Talmudist of the Syrkin line), 2
Skoropadskyi, Pavlo, 131n78
Slobodinskaia (née Beizer), Tema, vii, 6, 27, 142–143
Slutsker, Yoshe-Iche (Iosif), 52, 84
socialist realism, 51n27
Soviet-Finnish War (*also known as* the Winter War), 4, 26, 136n86
Soyer, Daniel, 10
St. Petersburg, vi, 7, 30n1–2, 125n66, 127n69
Starkova, K. B., 72n45
Starodub, 52, 88
Surazh District, 2–3, 69
Surazh, 2, 35, 62
Syrkin family, 2, 34. *See also* Sirkis, Yoel

T
Tankhil'-Tankhilevich, Pavel, 4n16
Trotsky, Leon, 4n16

U
Unecha, 4n16

V
VChK (the All-Russian Extraordinary Commission for the Struggle against Counterrevolution and Sabotage), 21, 135

W
War Communism, 1918–1922, 4n12
World War I, 9, 20, 126–127
World War II, 5, 9, 16, 22, 30n2, 53n28, 136n87

Y
YIVO, vi, 10,
Yukhnev, Andrei, vi
Yukhneva, Ekaterina, vi
Yukhneva, Natalia Vasilievna, vi

Z
Zeltser, Arkadi, vi, 74n46
Zionism, 20, 39n12, 69n39, 84
Zionist-Socialists, 84
Zlotina, Khaia-Reize, 24, 116n62, 138n92

www.ingramcontent.com/pod-product-compliance
Lightning Source LLC
Chambersburg PA
CBHW070614170426
43200CB00012B/2688